J. W. Rongiel.
Jan 1972.

Also by Ralph Wightman

TAKE LIFE EASY

THE COUNTRYSIDE TODAY

Wallace's Ground

Ralph Wightman

PELHAM BOOKS

First published in Great Britain by
PELHAM BOOKS LTD
52 *Bedford Square*
*London, W.C.*1
1971

7207 0442 1

Set and printed in Great Britain by
Tonbridge Printers Ltd, Peach Hall Works, Tonbridge, Kent
in Baskerville eleven on twelve point on paper supplied by
P. F. Bingham Ltd, and bound by James Burn
at Esher, Surrey

Contents

Chapter One

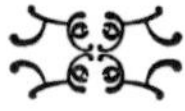

Something Solid

Wallace's Ground is a very ordinary field in Dorset. On the Ordnance Survey map of my native village it appears as No. 232, 13.861 acres. My immediate reaction to the word 'home' is to think of this plot of land rather than of parents, or of the house in which I was born. This is probably because both my parents have been dead for many years, and their home has been pulled down to straighten a bend in the village street.

All people have different responses to the word 'home'. In fact enquiries have shown that to many it is nothing to do with the past or the future, but is the present environment of those they love. To them home is something they have made themselves out of attempts to be kind, honest and generous. This feeling usually goes with the widespread substitution of religion, by what is generally called 'humanism'.

Humanists are very frequently highly moral and pleasant people. They can be envied for their ability to stand alone, with no reliance on a God and a future life, which both go on 'from everlasting to everlasting.' Perhaps it is a weakness to need to lean on something outside oneself. The late A. G. Street felt the need when he referred to 'Land Everlasting', and this is similar to my own regard for the phrase 'abiding things'. Then, although he was not a Christian, Thomas Hardy felt the need for things which 'go onward the same'.

This has always meant Wallace's Ground for me, although it did not exist as a field before the Enclosure Acts of the late eighteenth or the early nineteenth centuries. What is more, it has changed fundamentally at least twice in my lifetime.

Presumably Mr Wallace was a former tenant, and he might well have been Mr Wallis. Names in the country pass on by word of mouth, and on official documents it is more usual to use Ordnance Survey numbers than names. Spelling, too, is always a bit uncertain, but in Dorset it is common to attach the occupier's name to a field. My Father rented Beck's Bottom, Smart's Field, and Baker's Mead. He knew the men who once farmed them, but had no memory of Wallace, so I do not even know its history.

To some countrymen the Dorset word 'Ground' used for 'field' may be unusual. *The Concise Oxford Dictionary* does not give it, except in the special sense of 'enclosed land for ornamental or recreation attached to a house'. It was when looking up this dictionary that I found ground defined as 'something solid'.

Something solid is what Wallace's Ground means to me. This includes home, land everlasting, the abiding things, and going onward the same. It means much more than just a field in Dorset. It is in some ways a symbol in which I need to trust.

The certainty of the truth of Christianity is renewed for me in the solitude of this plot of earth, and I am very sure about Christ. This is no virtue, and it may be a weakness to need something as a support. I know many unbelievers who lead far better lives, and some people might well wonder how a professed Christian can reconcile his belief with his behaviour. This has often been quoted as a reason for not accepting the Faith. Possibly most Christians are conscious that their faults cause doubts in others, but this has very little to do with their own trust in the Grace of God on all their sins, and their need for sure belief.

G. K. Chesterton expressed much of what I mean in his poem 'A Second Childhood'. He describes the wonder of 'carpets of the grass' and of God's mercy. He saw the mystery in ordinary things, such as night and day. For me the wonder is in an ordinary field, a ground, which is something solid.

'Strange the plain things are' is a line of poetry which conveys the essence of what I am having the greatest difficulty in explaining. Only poets can use words of one syllable and leave the rest of us convinced that we know almost what they mean. It is probably safer to forget anything mystic that Wallace's Ground means to me, and leave it at the plain fact that I like this pleasant, unspectacular field.

In the last few years there has been a growing realisation of how small men are in relation to the universe. Of course we have all accepted and believed certain facts from the scientists. The earth as a round ball has been familiar in the globes of thousands of school classrooms. We smiled tolerantly about our ancestors who were convinced that the earth was flat, yet till very recently there was nothing in our daily lives that was inconsistent with living on a fairly flat surface.

The effect of films of the earth taken from the moon were a shock to most reasonably intelligent people. We had seen so many globes in geography lessons, and, suddenly, here was a picture of a real globe in the vast emptiness of space.

As they returned did the lunar travellers feel glad to approach this familiar huge earth, with only the slight curve of the horizon of the vast ocean to remind them that it is only a round speck of infinity? To me the sight of that tiny ball brought back memories of a radio programme which I once helped to write about Wallace's Ground in 1947.

We called it 'A Field in Dorset', and the opening thought came from the producer, Brandon Acton-Bond. He saw the earth 'spinning on its axis'. The continents and seas came into sunlight and returned to darkness. Descending, it was possible to spot Europe, then England, and so to the pattern of the great Peninsula of the South West. Lower the land becomes recognisable, 'the pendant Portland Bill and piled up Chesil Beach mark unmistakable Dorset'. He goes on 'Confine the scene further . . . Here is the chalky, flinty land of the hill tops around Piddletrenthide and here – to make the picture even smaller – here is this one field.'

Obviously Brandon was able to imagine what I only experienced in 1969. My first draft of an introduction had been much more earthbound. I had gone eight miles north of Piddletrenthide to the highest hill on our Dorset chalk, called Bulbarrow. I wrote, 'It is not an exceedingly high mountain.

In fact is is not a mountain at all, but the view from the top does give the impression of seeing the kingdoms of the earth and the glory of them.'

My feeling was that England is very small, and yet much too big for one man to know it all. The County of Dorset is small, but again much too big for intimate knowledge. 'Perhaps one field is too big, but let us look at just one field.'

That was my first approach to describing Wallace's Ground. It is now possible to realise the insignificance of the world, but I think I still end by wondering if one field is too much to comprehend.

The chalk hills seldom provide any scenery which takes your breath away. They never make you feel insignificant, as high mountains can. There is nothing magnificent about the little clear streams to compare with the waterfalls on Helvellyn after a thunderstorm, or the little Lyn River in spate, dashing amongst the boulders on Exmoor. Equally there is nothing sleepy about them, as there is in some broad rivers of East Anglia, where it is difficult to see which way they are flowing.

The chalk is comfortable country, and at the same time it is bracing. The endless chatter of the brooks in the valleys takes away any feeling of oppressive weariness on still hot days, and there is always a little breeze on the hills. Conversely, in winter, there may be a blizzard on the bare, highest land on the farm, but it suddenly loses its power when you reach a hedge. What is more the climate changes suddenly as you drop steeply down the lane to the village. There is 'two coats' difference between the garden of the farmhouse, and the more exposed parts of Wallace's Ground.

That 'two coats difference' is a pleasant Dorset saying, which is quite understandable about human beings exposed at 500 feet or sheltered only 100 yards away at 200 feet. What differences there must be for plants and animals on one side or other of a hedge. Even more, how utterly the climate must change for tinier creatures in thick grass or underground. Science has done some work on this sort of significant difference in the climate of a few inches of depth, and its effect on living creatures. When we think of a world whose boundaries are confined to inches, the 13.861 acres of Wallace's Ground are as large as the lunar photographs made space appear.

Perhaps it is necessary to realise this in trying to comprehend one field. Yet as a beginning it is worth taking in the appeal of a landscape which is by no means a beauty spot. The fact that looking up at the chalk hills produces no feeling of human insignificance is only half the truth. The man who climbs to the top of the ridges does not look down as a god on the trivial dwellings of his neighbours. There is neither depression of spirit nor arrogance in this land of gentle slopes, but best of all, there is no monotony.

As a boy I remember how difficult it was to find a football pitch in our narrow valleys, or on the plateau of the hills between the streams. In fact until I left home for boarding school on a different soil, my image of a sports field had the goals in the lower part, with a pronounced slope up to the touch lines on either side. Which means it was quite a definite shallow valley, where the wingers found it easy to put over a centre.

During the 1939 war I found how truly my own village was typical of the belt of chalk which crosses Dorset. A new airfield was urgently needed, which meant flat land, and also dry land. There was no time for drainage, or for clearing trees, which would both be necessary on big stretches of the flat clay area of Dorset's larger vales. The chalk hills were dry, there were very few trees, and huge fields meant little uprooting of hedges. The trouble was that those of us who knew the farms of the county intimately could not think of any sizeable area of flat plateau. The Forces made a plane available, and we did find one farm which was just acceptable, but it was a strange experience to peer down, searching for a few hundred level acres, in a hundred square miles of small hills.

To me the cliff faces of high mountains get more frightening with my increasing age. Modern art is almost completely outside the appreciation of normal men, but sometimes it seems to bring out the differences between our appreciation of country scenery. An abstract of straight lines, acute angles and vivid contrasting colours is for the mountaineer. My taste would be the picture of gentle curves with smooth blending of greens and pale blues. I do not want to live with a painting which is not as recognisable a picture as is a photograph. But if it had to be a choice of abstracts between straight lines and curves, there is no doubt which I should take.

The first experience of a baby starts with soft, warm curves. In spite of fashion models the young man turns instinctively to the same gentle slopes. Indeed it may be that the skinniest of models support the argument. They are never really angular, and many of us like miniature curves more than aggressive jutting hills.

Whatever the artist or the physiologist may make of it, the charm of chalk country lies first in its infinite but smooth variety. The next attribute is the chance it offers of solitude without loneliness. The village of Piddletrenthide is typical of most of the settlements on the chalk of Dorset. A small stream has cut a narrow valley through the chalk. For at least a thousand years every house and shed for animals has been near the stream. A parallel stream ran down similar steep-sided valleys at a distance of three to five miles to east and west. In between is a plateau of gently rolling land all flat enough to plough.

The solitude without loneliness arises because the ploughing and cropping of the hill fields speaks of human presence, although nearly every building is out of sight in the deep valleys. From Wallace's Ground it is possible to look over three hamlets without seeing any sign of them. The view is of a dozen miles of gently undulating land, with little sign of life except for the crops. The few buildings are fairly new storage barns for straw and grain, or relics from the end of the last century which had been erected from secondhand materials.

The almost complete absence of houses was due to the fact that pumping drinking water through pipes did not spread to villages and farms until after the 1914–18 war. The stream was used to water dairy cows in the valley, and human dwellings either had a well just inside or outside the house. Alternatively, half a dozen houses might share a communal well for drinking water, whilst dipping buckets of water from the stream for washing purposes. The village pump was a reality, and since men fetched a couple of bucketsfull every evening after work, it was a natural centre for gossip. The house of my birth was forty yards from the pump, but the back wall of the house rose straight from the stream. There was a bridge from the back door across the stream to the vegetable plot on the other side. From this bridge water was dipped for baths and laundry, whilst all liquid refuse was thrown from it into the river.

Before 1914 a few of the larger houses were pumping from their private well to a tank in the roof. They also had a water-closet, and a drain which took all liquid straight into the stream. Since only four houses in the two miles of straggling village had any form of drain, the pollution was not very serious. Drainage from cowstalls, horse stables and piggeries went the same way, but usually via a farm yard. The yard held a lot of straw and the aim was to soak up liquid effluent to make good dung. Washing cows or cowstall floors was quite unknown, and there were no detergents. A fast flowing stream cleanses itself fairly quickly, and the inhabitants tried to save anything with a fertilising value, even although they had never heard of the evils of pollution.

Looking back it is fairly certain that larger villages, such as Cerne Abbas in the next valley had more outbreaks of disease than Piddletrenthide. At the time none of us thought it had anything to do with the greater fouling of their stream. Perhaps there was no connection, since both rivers carried a fair number of trout, and shoals of minnows. These were greatly reduced when hygiene led to washing cows, and humans used a great many detergents and disinfectants.

All this seems a long way from the little hills and Wallace's Ground. It actually had a big influence on the buildings on the hills, and the view from the top. There could be no cottages outside the valley, and cows yielding milk need to drink twice daily. The obvious place for sheds was adjoining the brook. Then pig-keeping on any substantial scale was always associated with cows. There was no sale for liquid milk except within a few miles of a large town, or near a railway station which would take churns to a city. In remote Dorset all milk was turned into butter or cheese, which meant there was skim milk or whey available for pigs. Hence the piggeries adjoined the cowsheds in the valley .

Through all the centuries the only source of soil fertility had been animal dung. The cows, the pigs and the horses in the valley provided substantial amounts. This had to be carted up the hills to the relatively flat plough land on top. It took three good horses to pull a load, which had been lifted from the 'mixen' laboriously by hand fork. When it reached the hill top it had to be spread by hand fork, all of which involved a great deal of time and effort. No one grudged this, and labour was very cheap, but there simply was not enough dung to fertilise the wide acres of hill land.

The other source of dung was the sheep, and the sheep had several advantages. Like deer and hares it could get enough water for its needs from succulent herbage, especially when wet with dew or rain. In addition crops could be grown for sheep, such as turnips, and 100 lb. of turnips contain 9 gallons of water. The sheep was only likely to need water when it was suckling a lamb, or a twin of lambs. Turnips or mangolds were available all the winter, so that was the best time for suckling to take place. This is precisely what happened on the chalk hills. All the farms to be seen from Wallace's Ground had flocks of sheep. These were white-faced Dorset Horns, lambing in October, or black-faced Downs lambing in January. They needed no water, and they were never housed, so there were no buildings on the hill.

Earlier I said there were a few relics of buildings from the last century. They were often a mile from the valley and village, and were in use well within living memory. In fact I knew an old bricklayer who put up one set of these buildings, about a hundred years ago, and they were in use until after the First War. They consisted of a cottage, a large barn, a pond, and a big yard. The whole was surrounded by a screen of trees for shelter, plus thick hedges of damsons.

The whole idea was to keep cattle on the hills so that

extra dung could be made on the spot where it was needed. They were to supplement sheep manure, not to replace it. There could be no question of keeping milking cows, because they would need more water than growing youngsters. The usual procedure was to buy strong heifers, get them in calf, and sell them as soon as they calved to dairy farmers in the clay vales. They could drink from the pond, which was fed by deep cart ruts converging on the buildings. This meant that the buildings were not on the very crest of the hill, but on a gentle slope a few hundred yards from the ridge. Ponds fed from cart ruts were also found in other fields away from the buildings, and there was one in a corner of Wallace's Ground, which was shared by two adjoining fields.

Up at the buildings the family in the cottage relied for drinking and washing water on a large tank which was fed from the tiled cottage roof. This tank was open to the sky and the water became rusty and smelly in anything approaching a drought. The only thing that can be said for it was that it was soft. In fact labourers who lived at hill buildings claimed to be relatively free from rheumatism. It now seems a high price to pay for being a mile from a road, and being unable to wash in a summer drought.

The barn at hill buildings was to hold grain threshed from surrounding fields, and straw stacks provided food and bedding for the yarded cattle. Our set was always called Pat's Castle, or sometimes Rat's Castle. No origin is known for the name and although Pat's is used on the Ordnance Survey map, I think Rat's Castle was more likely and appropriate. No Pat ever owned it, and the builder's name was George. Nothing now remains of the cottage and not much of the barn. All that persists is the encircling trees against the skyline and a few sloe and damson bushes. Water comes to the hill in a pipe, and chemical fertilisers have removed some of the absolute necessity for cow dung.

Occasionally hill buildings of the type described had two cottages and a horse stable. The second cottage housed the ploughman, and the horses were spared the mile long journey from the valley to the more remote hill tops. This arrangement was apt to put a heavy strain on the supply of rain water in the pond and in the storage tanks. In addition ploughmen were higher in the social scale than the general labourer, who had little responsible work with the in-calf heifers. There was no skill required in throwing out straw and mangolds to feed them. When calving started he merely reported at once to the farmer or foreman, although like most countrymen he was capable of assisting straight-forward cases. He then had to see the calf take its first swig of milk, and milk out any surplus. Within days the new mother and child would be taken to market, and, with a weekly market, he never had to milk any heifer for more than nine days.

The labourer who lived on the hill was often not highly intelligent, whereas the carter was skilled, and likely to leave a farm where his wife had to live in such isolation. The shepherd was then the most highly paid of workers, and he too refused to live in such a place, even though it was much nearer his work. The inhabited hill buildings were started soon after the land was split into fields, say between 1770 and 1830. Most of the cottages had fallen down before piped water was available about 1930, which was also before farm ruts had been made possible for tough cars. It was a short life for a farming system.

The other type of hill building with no cottage attached was also put up to keep non-milking cattle on the hills, and for the same reason of providing extra dung. Their date was a bit later, about 1870, with a depression in full blast. They consisted of a shed with one side opening to a straw yard. They were built of old railways sleepers and second-hand corrugated iron. Water was collected in a tank from the roof, and there was a pond in the fence which separated this ugly collection of shacks from Wallace's Ground.

It may seem strange to stress the importance of dung for growing crops, whereas obviously keeping cattle on the hill meant that several fields, such as Wallace's Ground had to be in pasture, in spite of the fact that they were flat enough to plough. The explanation is that farming prices had fallen very low after 1860, when a flood of grain from America was reaching the country. Meat was not affected, until refrigeration became common, which was several years later.

Milk and milk products were even less dominated by imports. This meant that keeping animals had become more profitable than growing grain. The dung was still needed for fertility, but it was increasingly used on grassland for hay rather than for corn.

In addition little was known about sowing grass and clover to form a pasture. Much of the growth of grass and clover was natural, which had taken a long time to improve by dunging, grazing and trimming with a mower. Landowners only let land with fierce penalties in the agreement against ploughing pasture. When war came, in 1914 and 1939 the Government had to order farmers to plough fields for grain growing. This protected the tenant against the no ploughing clause in his agreement. At the same time landlords were promised compensation after the wars if they could prove loss arising from breaking grassland. Fortunately, by 1918 there was a fairly widespread knowledge of seeds available, and by 1945 scientists were teaching that the best way to improve old pasture was to plough it up and reseed. Landlords no longer feared their land would be less profitable to let or sell if it was arable.

My first memory of Wallace's Ground, however, was of a grass field. In fact the food shortage in the first World War did not develop until fairly late in the conflict. Much less pasture was ordered to be ploughed than in the last war, and the Authorities were inclined merely to tell the farmer what extra acreage they expected him to crop, leaving the choice of field to him. On my Father's farm, which was all ploughable, we chose to break a 32 acre field of very poor pasture. The better grassland, including Wallace's Ground, was left unploughed until the second war.

Hence through all my childhood and up to middle age, this field, this symbol of home for me was either carrying sheep, or heifers, or being cut for hay. In the light of present knowledge it was not very productive pasture. It grew daisies, which are a sign of poverty, and of over-grazing, but I did not know this as a small boy. One of my earliest memories was of four of us, threee boys and a girl, all under 8 years of age, sitting in the warm sun and making daisy chains.

The reason for the memory was that in the complete innocence of childhood the talk turned to the difference between girls and boys. The girl was very interested in seeing our private parts, but did not expose her own. This was absolutely all. There was no physical contact. None of us had been told the facts of life, and we were all far too young to be more than vaguely interested. Even although as country children we must have seen animals copulating, it had meant nothing to us. In fact I doubt if it ever does to any child until puberty. This episode is remembered because we had been seen, and our elders became very excited. We had apparently committed a very serious sin, but no one gave us anything remotely resembling an explanation. We were forbidden to do it again, but our interest was so slight that even this ban did not tempt us to repeat the offence. It was memorable because it had caused such a stir. As far as I know we all grew up without any abnormal twists in our thoughts and behaviour. In my own case the only effect is a feeling that sex education of the young is not wildly important at an early age. Instead polite behaviour must be taught with no great need for explanation, just as children are taught not to drink tea from a saucer, with no reason provided.

Other early memories were of picking mushrooms in the dawn of autumn days. The grass was wet with dew and my feet were cold. Rubber boots had not been invented, and very few of leather were completely waterproof. Unfortunately the whole village knew that the field grew mushrooms, so that the discomfort of chilly feet was not always rewarded with a good breakfast. In addition the whole village was inhabited by people closely connected with farming. Today, when four-fifths of the parishioners are town born it is sometimes possible to bluff them from entering a field. Recently a neighbour put a few dry cows in his mushroom ground and erected a notice 'Beware of the Bull'. All his dairy is artificially inseminated, and he had not kept a bull for years, but the warning worked. My generation would never have mistaken a cow for a bull. They also knew that a real bull was very unlikely to be dangerous if the dog was left at home and the mushroom picker disregarded the bull and his wives.

The shape of Wallace's Ground is rectangular with a length four times its breadth, and it has a distinct slope to the south at one end and a much steeper fall eastward at the other. For the chalk hills, though, this is reasonably flat, and as children we played cricket and football on it. Much later the Parish Council made it a village sports ground, and fenced one third of it off with a wire fence. My Father retained the right to graze but was forbidden to plough. This was the first revolution I remember in the field.

For no very clear reason organised sport in the village was not very popular, or it may be that the quarter mile steep rough lane from the main road put off would-be players. Our neighbours, in a much smaller village, still run a team in a local league and our lads may have joined them. At any rate, in the 1960s the Parish Council returned the playing field portion for normal farming. Ever since it has been ploughed for crops or sown to grass for a few years. This cultivation of the whole field is the second revolution in Wallace's Ground, but it still remains my solid abiding thing.

In it I have seen vast changes in farming machinery, and in the use of chemical fertilisers and pesticides. The pond in the corner is silted up, but there is abundant drinking water in a trough fed by a mains supply. When the field is growing corn the crops are good, much better than when my Brother first ploughed part of it in 1942. The rough lane, with its one in seven gradient from the village, has been surfaced to make a perfectly good road for tractors and cars. When the field is sown for a few years to grass and clover, the herbage is thick and productive. The daisies have vanished, yet the look of the field is much as it always has been in my lifetime.

If there are sheep in the field they will all have white faces and horns in both sexes. This is the same breed that my Father kept, and only an expert would notice that they are now more compact, more shapely, and less leggy. The Ground is too far from the milking shed for cows to walk to and fro for grazing, but there may well be yearlings, or in-calf heifers. These are all black-and-white Friesians, whereas Father preferred red Devons – the rubies of the West – or red and white Shorthorns. Entering the field and sitting on the grass will almost certainly result in an age-old reaction from the sheep and cattle. They have a curiosity which is much greater than any suspicion they may feel about strangers. If you sit silently and motionless both sheep and cattle will approach, first to sniffing distance, and then to licking. One very good reason for not driving a car through the gate is that licking by heifers is distinctly tough on the paint.

I have played in this field, and done most ordinary forms of work here. The high arts of hurdle making and thatching are beyond me, but I have tried my hand at both to a point that I can appreciate just what an expert is doing. This is possibly more important than it sounds. The sad thing about the gulf between town and country is the fact that the best of good-natured outsiders does not really see the things he finds pleasant. I have been teased quite often by city friends for glancing over a hedge, while driving a car, and saying 'Nice bunch of heifers.' They see a picturesque collection of bovine animals, but not the virtues of the individual in the group. In fact I have been completely disbelieved for saying a shepherd learns to know every animal in his flock, much quicker than a headmaster gets to recognise the 300 boys in his school.

I have also been teased for looking at a photograph of the countryside and saying 'Ah that is decent chalk.' Actually the smooth curves of the chalk are unmistakable to anyone who knows anything about the shape of the land, which is caused by the rock underneath it. As for 'decent', well perhaps that is being used in an old-fashioned way meaning 'kind'.

The soil of Wallace's Ground is kind. It never soaked with water to excess. It seldom dries right out, and never cracks. There is always shelter under one or other of the hedges. In this field I have worked as a small boy, doing trivial jobs, such as leading the horses in laden wagons at haymaking time. Later I have worked with strong men, and kept up with them all day as an equal. In the nature of things I must have made mistakes and been ticked off. Yet the memory of working in a team is that my fellows were 'decent' meaning kind.

Wallace's Ground is something solid, on the decent chalk.

Chapter Two

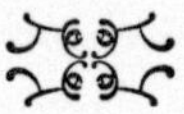

Death or Sleep

Winter in Wallace's Ground has never felt like death to me, and I do not think it ever will. This is one reason for being thankful for a country upbringing, because to townsmen past middle age there is often a feeling of doom about winter. The young will cheerfully agree that everyone will eventually die, but I think I was over 55 before I started genuinely realising that it would inevitably happen to me.

It is only the elderly who see winter as death, and the city dweller has far less in the way of comfortable sights and sounds than I have always had in our native fields. A dead bush is utterly different from a sleeping shrub. Even if snow comes, and a barren wind sweeps over the hill, there will be sounds of life as soon as the blizzard stops. In the long nights it is never more than a matter of hours before darkness ends. It all makes it much easier to believe that death like winter is sleep – a pause before new life. I am very grateful that I can look at the leafless hedges, and see the buds. That I can hear the short burst of song from a robin, and the swish of wings as the peewits wheel over the valley. That I know the meaning of the marks which appear very soon after the snow stops falling, when foxes, rabbits, rats and birds show that life remains.

All this has been a comfort from Wallace's Ground, which I have only needed or noticed in very recent years. To the young there is no fear of winter, and bitter cold experiences leave no mark. The care of animals in winter must have been actively painful on many occasions, yet I have to make an effort to remember the dreary days of endless rain, in an age when protective clothing was primitive. We had no rubber boots and I did not possess enough leather boots to be sure of a dry pair several times daily. The farm workers with only one pair must have gone for months with wet feet. Rubber boots make holes in socks, but the countryman lives in them, or in the newer polythene type, and is at least dry. The type of coats and hats worn by seamen known as 'south westers' kept out the wet, but they were stiff and confining for hard work such as carrying hurdles. They were also terribly liable to tear or crack. There was something to be said for the plentiful supply of old sacks available on most farms, for keeping out rain or cold. Modern plastic bags are not as good.

We must have been highly uncomfortable at best, and in danger of such things as frostbite on some occasions. Winter was a real cause of dread, but the young still seem to have no fear, and the old have the protection of faulty memories. My recollections are of sliding every year on frozen ponds, of the horses hauling an improvised snow plough, and of great, blazing, log fires in the evening. True winter weather in Wallace's Ground can only be remembered accurately with the help of a book by an old friend. It is *Agricultural Records A.D. 220–1968* by a Wiltshire farmer, J. M. Stratton.

To the farmer winter is usually December, January and February, if we think of these as months when plant growth ceases, and it is unwise to sow crops. Actually the dates will vary. Grass grows in favoured parts of Devon all the year, in perhaps four years out of five. In addition grain can often be sown in February on the chalk soils of the Southern Counties. Consulting Mr Stratton's book about my young days I could not have done much sliding on icy ponds in 1907, but it was cold in 1908, 1909 and 1910 with snow in March in 1908. The 1911 winter was dull and damp, and the next very cold spell was in 1917. Obviously my 'good old-fashioned winters' occurred just about as infrequently as they have in the last ten years. The same goes for really heavy snow in Southern England. I can only remember when roads were seriously blocked in 1941, 1942, 1947, 1956 and 1963.

These dates seem to make nonsense of some widely held beliefs, such as that Dorset gets a hard winter about one year in ten. Similar facts for dry harvests indicate that we may only get an average of one in ten, but they are not evenly spaced. All my nostalgic thoughts about sliding on the pond in Wallace's Ground and of having picnics in the hot hay fields, could only have been true occasionally. Moreover there was and is no pattern in the weather. The harvest of 1968 was very bad at home, and the harvest of 1969 was very good. It is rather like tossing a coin. The average of a multitude of tosses may be an equal number of heads and of tails, but there is nothing to stop, say, twenty tails in succession. As to memories, like sundials they 'only record the sunny hours'.

Farming is very dependant on the weather, and methods are based on the average of weather in different parts of the country. East Anglia has a low average rainfall and South West England a high one. Thus growing crops is common even on heavy soils in the East, and is mainly confined to quick drying soils in the South West. Every now and then the climate is dry in the West and extremely wet in the East. The wet autumn and winter of 1968–69 meant that thousands of acres in East Anglia could not be sown at all, whereas Wallace's Ground gave an excellent crop in 1969. This will not stop East Anglia from continuing to cultivate difficult soils, nor interfere with my nephew's plan of sowing temporary grass for his cows in very friendly, easy land. The average climate does influence farming, not the exceptions.

There is a sense in which this rectangular field has not changed although I have known it look wildly different in permanent pasture, and in arable. It has kept fattening cattle, rearing youngsters, cows, sheep and even poultry. At one time we considered tethering sows, and using semi-circular, corrugated iron shelters. This never happened but the Ground would have been quite suitable for the job. Greatest change of all was the spell when part of it was taken as a sports field. It has altered in appearance to an extent which must seem to the stranger the reverse of abiding. Yet it has always worked well within its capacities.

There is nothing steep about it, but even in the centre you cannot look round and see all of every hedge. The slopes do not stop easy ploughing, and the soil is not sticky. It grows good corn and fair grass, but I cannot imagine it in carrots, or onions, or grapes. Unfortunately I could imagine it under bungalows, but that is nothing to do with the capacity of the Field. These hang on slope, soil and climate.

Possible new methods may enable farmers to override the influence of climate.

There are hopes that artificially drying grass might become cheap enough to cut out other forms of conserving herbage for winter use. At present haymaking is still a risk, and so is the increasing custom of silage making. The latter is packing green, or slightly wilted herbage under some form of seal to keep out the air. Wallace's Ground has been used for hay and for silage, but so far not for dried grass. My winter memories of the field in grass are of feeding hay to rams, or silage to cattle.

In both cases the animals had their bulky food spread in small heaps, and only when they were getting grain or cattle cake was it placed in troughs. They were eager enough for hay or silage, but much more excited at the prospect of spicy cake. Our Dorset Horn sheep are tame enough, but the rams have very massive curled horns. I remember feeding half a dozen rams once, and being careless in turning my back on one of them. He butted me on the behind, and it lifted me off the ground, although it was probably not malicious, but merely a friendly prod.

The domestic animals in Wallace's Ground are utterly dependent on man, especially in winter.

This has always been the case in enclosed fields, and the nearest thing to a natural life for animals is for sheep on unfenced high mountains, or for ponies on open country of such places as the New Forest. Cattle and sheep in my favourite field have always been dominated by humans, but to a casual visitor they may often have seemed to be free. They were certainly in the good, open air, and the cattle could roam at will over 13 acres of grass. Sometimes the sheep were penned behind hurdles when the Ground was growing turnips, or some other form of winter vegetation. They could only wander over a restricted patch each day, but it was in the open air. However small their daily fold they were able to move more freely than hens in cages, or calves in pens too small to allow them to turn round.

It is extremely difficult to define just what is humane in the treatment of farm livestock. The plea for access to the open air is not as simple as it sounds. Plenty of wild creatures avoid the open air in winter, and the most primitive of human beings are known to have crowded into caves before they invented the building of shelters. Some animals build their own caves, and use them only in bad weather. The hole of a rabbit, or a mole, or a badger or a fox offers very restricted quarters and darkness. They can certainly go to the open air at will, but badgers choose to be snug for days on end when a blizzard is raging.

Animals have coats designed to protect them from cold and damp. If men bring sheep indoors for the winter less wool is produced, and indoor cattle grow less shaggy hair. This may mean that nature intended them to live in the open, but it is no sort of proof that they are unhappy or uncomfortable under a roof.

Real life in the wild is often very cruel, and always extremely wasteful. How many robins die every year to maintain a fairly stable population? Keeping animals for human food, or for wool, or for leather cannot be carried on unless a surplus are kept alive every season. The sheep on the mountains, and the ponies in the New Forest have been mentioned as living near nature. In both there is a danger of death in winter from starvation. The hill sheep may end the year with 70 lambs from 100 ewes. This low figure is partly due to the death of weakly lambs soon after birth, and partly to a considerable amount of infertility in the ewes. The same sheep on lowland grass might almost double this lambing percentage. The small number of lambs from the hills is more lack of food than of exposure, but with 70 per cent lambs there is still a surplus if the ewes live more than one year. In real wild life deaths usually roughly balance survival.

Wallace's Ground is upland, about half-way between hill and lowland. It can be bleak, but seldom for the length of time that real winter brings to the mountains. In a 13 acre field the ewes can be seen with ease, and food provided to meet their needs. Infertility is not a problem, and the death rate of very young lambs is much lower than in high, open country. Yet it is probably not an exaggeration to say that 10 per cent of lambs born die within the first fortnight. Is this loss inevitable or could more lambs be saved if the ewes were housed in winter?

If the ewes were housed in winter, conditions for the shepherd would be much more comfortable. In addition it would be possible to reduce lamb deaths by early attention, and by artificially feeding orphans and triplets, or even twins. It would be necessary to change to something a little more prolific than mountain breeds, but possible to look forward to 200 lambs sold per 100 ewes. Disease risks would be increased by crowded conditions indoors, and there would be none of the exercise which has always been considered necessary for breeding ewes. Actually the need for exercise has had no research done on it as far as I know.

A sheep house in Wallace's Ground is a possibility for the future. It would mean extra expense in taking hay and other foods to the animals. A new building would cost something, although only rough shelter is necessary, not the elaborate climate control provided for hens. There would be a slightly lower production of wool and the need for more food. It is surprising how much nutriment sheep manage to nibble when roaming over what seems to be very bare winter pasture.

An advantage not always realised is that if sheep are kept off pasture for months the herbage will not be soiled by their droppings. This will mean that more ewes and lambs can be kept per acre, especially if the pasture is treated to grow extra grass with chemical fertiliser. Higher production per acre is an essential in profitable farming, but is often limited by an increase in disease where animals are crowded. This danger from crowding is true about the human animal, but in many cases disease prevention has advanced much further with man than with animals. In particular this is true of what could be called visible parasites.

Invisible forms of life still cause plenty of illness in humans, as for instance the common cold, but in civilised countries it is unusual to hear of men suffering from large internal worms. I have known one man in my life who had tape worms in his stomach, and have heard of a few score of cases of liver fluke. With domestic animals it would be more true to say that it is unusual for them to get through life without some degree of infection with visible parasites.

'Worms' is a bad word to use because it is immediately connected in the mind with earth worms, and the visible parasites of animals do not always have a wormy shape. The fluke has been described as shaped like a flat fish. The tape worm resembles a piece of tape, feet long, and consisting of separate sections which break off from the tape as they ripen. There are several round stomach worms which vary from an inch or more of thin, twisted string, to shorter, very fine threads only just visible. The lung worm is two to three inches long and about half-way between thread and very fine string.

In some cases the life history of the pest is very complicated, but almost always there is a stage when it is coughed up, or more often leaves the body in the dung. In other words the transfer from one animal to another is via the grass. The risk of picking up dangerous numbers is that a large concentration of animals is grazing on land which has been recently soiled with dung. Some parasites may survive on the soil for a year, but a vast number die in a few months. Hence winter housing of ewes means the pasture is relatively clean when the lambs go out in spring, and it is the lambs which are in most danger. Adult ewes seem to develop some immunity from stomach worms, but they can infect the pasture for the lambs.

It is a strange experience to lean on the gate of Wallace's Ground and to realise that millions of parasites may be on the pleasant blades of grass. Most of them are invisible in their life-stage outside the sheep, but the liver fluke can be just seen as tiny white specks, smaller than a pin's head. Lambs will be playing happily, especially between April showers, but death may threaten as they start eating grass to supplement their mother's milk.

With this in mind there might well be justification for a sheep house in Wallace's Ground, even if it is made of untidy, second-hand materials. The ewes do not need the shelter at this unimportant height of upland. They lie in the hoar frost on a winter morning, quietly chewing the cud, and contentedly breathing a trace of mist on the cold air. When the gate slams as a sign of the arrival of breakfast hay, they get up and crowd to the cribs. Behind them green patches in the white field are the shape of their bodies, and show they have not bothered to move in hours. No, the ewes can safely live in the open, but all the time they are contaminating the grass for the lambs in spring.

Actually the housing of sheep in Wallace's Ground is unlikely to happen unless the breed of sheep should be changed. For sixty years that breed has been the Dorset Horn, with the peculiar power amongst sheep of lambing in October instead of March. The whole point of housing under modern conditions is for the vast majority of sheep which lamb in spring, just as the grass is beginning to grow. If sheep are off the pasture all the winter, there is no treading, no nibbling of grass, but best of all no soiling with parasites from dung. The autumn lambing of the Horn breeds means that any green food for them will have to come from crops of such things as kale, cabbage or turnips. Such crops will be grown on plough land, and will be almost certain to follow barley. Thus no sheep are likely to have dunged on the soil for at least two years, and the lambs are quite safe.

The growing of crops for winter grazing by sheep is tending to die out, because of the cost of moving the fence every day, to ration supplies, and to give even grazing. It is curious that before winter green crops were developed, about 150 years ago, the Dorset Horn sheep were housed in winter. This allowed the ewes to be fed generously on hay and oats to fatten their lambs for the luxury eating of the rich. William Cobbett, in 1820, referred to 'the white-faced, Dorset *house* lambs'.

Wallace's Ground, if left in grass, could infect sheep with lung worms, but it is quite safe from liver fluke because there are no swamps, and no wet patches or ditches where the particular water snail connected with fluke can breed. Sheep get water from dewy herbage, and this sufficed in summer when Dorset Horn ewes were not feeding lambs. In the winter, when Dorset Horn sheep are in full milk they need moisture, but they are then getting lush kale or watery turnips. It is a great relief to have Wallace's Ground free from liver fluke because cattle pick up quite as many as sheep on wet land, yet for some reason symptoms of illness are far less common. Possibly fluke in cattle may lead to reduced milk yields, poor quality milk and infertility. There is seldom the rapid loss of weight, and fatal pining, which are seen when sheep have large numbers of adult flukes in their livers. It is common for fat cattle, from wet land, to have rotten livers when slaughtered, with no sign of a check in their growth.

Perhaps it is less well known that fluke may infect the hare, the rabbit and man. In the case of humans uncooked green food must be the source, and this almost always means water-cress. Such cress is always from wild plants, growing by streams which have been soiled by sheep or cattle dung. The cultivated cress, sold by firms of repute, is completely safe. Each bunch is labelled with the name of the grower. The water is from deep spring or artesian wells, from which animals are rigidly excluded. Thus the water snail could certainly live in the cress beds, but safety is guaranteed because there is no danger of fluke reaching them from animal dung.

For three-quarters of my life I have picked and eaten wild cress with no suggestion of illness. This was before I heard fluke could attack humans, but I did know that green uncooked food in winter was an excellent addition to my diet. The latter fact remains true, and I eat more cress than in the past. It may be significant that the biggest demand for cress is in the North of England where the winters are long. Without any doubt city dwellers in the North will be wise to continue buying properly identified, cultivated cress. The danger is to country people who pick it from any stream. The greener and stronger it looks in such places the more likely it is that the water contains dung. The only other risk is that in the south wild cress may be sold to small shopkeepers who have never heard of disease, or hawked round a district by equally innocent gipsies.

Some of the satisfaction of looking at Wallace's Ground lies in the knowledge that it is healthy land as far as some very unpleasant diseases are concerned. Purchased sheep might contain fluke but could not pass it on. Then there are several diseases which are passed from one animal to another by blood sucking ticks. The tick itself does no harm in most cases, apart from causing irritation. It drops off sheep or cattle when it is gorged, and attaches itself to another when it wants more food. Thus it can mechanically convey diseases from one animal to another, just as fleas spread myxomatosis in rabbits. Fortunately, once more Wallace's Ground is reasonably safe. Ticks are fairly large, as big as peas, and can be seen easily by birds when they lie on the earth. The old permanent turf of the field and the modern short term leys are equal in offering little cover for ticks. Diseases carried by these pests are confined to rough grazing and neglected scrub land.

Leaning on the gate it is pleasant to remember some of the horrors we are spared, and thinking of foul diseases is not morbid. Wallace's Ground on a winter day can look very peaceful. There may be a jarring note from a fertiliser bag left carelessly on the hedge, but no visible sign of the pollution which is inescapable in cities. The air is pure and there is no stagnant water. When the Field has been ploughed for cropping it looks clean and empty of offence. When in pasture there is only a little mud near the gate, and the rest is innocent green. Every prospect pleases, and only a born countryman is likely to know that the turf is full of teeming life.

Millions of parasites and bacteria and viruses are living in that top few inches of soil. Winter checks the activity of most of them. Dung is preserved unchanged in periods of frost, but vanishes in days when the soil temperature is over 10 degrees C. It must have come as a wild surprise when men first realised that the decay of once living material is not part of death, but of crowding life. The complicated material of dead vegetable and animal bodies is changed back, by incredibly small and numerous living creatures to simple chemicals – to gas, water and traces of minerals. Later warmth and light will enable plants to build new complicated growth, but in dead winter the cycle slows and stops. There is no decay and no re-growth in frozen soil.

Unfortunately the plain and simple things are complicated by our climate. There is no predictable period for winter as there is on the wheat fields of Canada, where life stops. In Wallace's Ground it is slowed. The temperature of the soil may be too low for plants to grow, but underground soluble plant foods are still slowly made from old dead roots and animal dung. Costly soluble chemicals applied by the farmer last summer were not all used in autumn growth. Without any cap of ice the cold winter rain can soak into the soil, and carry plant food into the subsoil, beyond the reach of the deepest growing roots of spring.

I have sometimes walked in Wallace's Ground in shoes on Christmas Day, with no mud, no strong wind, and even some illusion of warmth in the sunshine. It has been impossible to wish for a long harsh winter, although our temperate, wet South of England does increase a loss of plant food into the subsoil, and to an increase in fertiliser bills. It also means that when real cold comes we are not prepared, and have probably taken slight precautions against snow. Fortunately farm workers are very quick to adapt themselves to an utterly new life.

In the old days of horses the first job was to take the teams to the blacksmith, where their smooth shoes were 'roughed'. This is the equivalent of fitting chains to the tyres of cars and tractors, but far more pleasant. Wrestling with cold chains is a horrible task even for the young and active. It was a good preparation for the wind on the hill to relax in a warm smithy whilst four mighty horses had their shoes roughened. They then moved confidently on the icy roads to haul hay to sheep and cattle.

Wallace's Ground in real cold is very familiar, but seldom do we have to settle into the 'utterly new life' mentioned above, because arctic conditions do not persist. The winter of 1963 will be quoted for a score of years, and the teen-agers will not believe the fireside tales of the elderly. Normally the ploughs are stopped for a day or two, and then the rain returns. Fortunately the soil of the Field is seldom too wet to plough. Recently the law has required strong cabs to be fitted over tractor seats, as a protection for the driver if the machine overturns. My nephew rigged up home-made cabs a dozen years ago to let the driver go on working in the rain. Only on such soils as that of the Ground is the comfort of the driver the limiting factor. Usually the soil rapidly becomes too wet and sticky to work.

Because it was so unusual, that shut down in 1963 is my most vivid memory of this favourite patch of earth in winter. It started on December 26th, 1962, and the final thaw did not come until March 4th. The beginning was light snow followed by a blizzard which choked the main road six feet deep in snow, but spared the lane to Wallace's Ground. Only two of the gates were blocked and this was no great problem for a tractor fitted with an improvised bull-dozer. On the first few days there was no great change in the usual life of the Field in winter. Nowhere on the farm could there be any cultivation, but the shepherd and head cowman needed help in shifting supplies of fodder for the animals. This was normal after a few inches of snow, but when the stuff persisted for months it was another story. With no chance of field work all the machinery on the farm had the best servicing in history.

The depth of the snow reminded me of old tales from my Father. There were certainly places where it was 'level with the hedges', to quote his phrase. We had far better tools for clearing it, but then there were far more urgent reasons for quick clearance. His village was practically self-sufficient, and so was the farm. It did not matter that it took a fort-night to dig by hand a single track road to Dorchester. He was not selling milk, and there was plenty of stored food for man and beast. My nephew had to get a dozen milk churns to the depot inside 24 hours, or face a heavy loss. It was done by disregarding roads and driving across country with a four-wheel-drive Land-Rover.

In Wallace's Ground there was some blowing of dry snow and some fresh falls, but the animals were perfectly happy. The biggest worry was when a water-pipe froze, and there was a day of feverish work with the temperature always below zero.

My main thrill was a partial thaw, followed by renewed cold in humid air. Hoar frost on the hedges of the field was familiar, and charming, but now we had every twig coated with ice. I believe this is called a 'silver thaw', and I have never seen anything more delicately lovely than the hedges of Wallace's Ground. The trees across the lane were as beautiful on a bigger scale.

It lasted three days, but then came tragedy. The weight of the ice was too much. In a keen wind every twig broke off, and many sizeable branches, so that beneath every tree and bush there was enough wood to be worth gathering for burning. The old ash trees across the lane suffered most, and when the real thaw came they looked like skeletons. It took several years for recovery, because all wood under three to four years of age had been torn from the trees. Even today it is possible to guess that at some time the ashes had a savage pruning.

The coldest night was January 18th, when we had what was then termed 40 degrees of frost, or minus 8 degrees F., when on average our coldest night in the Field shows 20 degrees F., which is cold enough for me. In fact, although Wallace's may average about forty-five night frosts per annum, the average day and night temperature in January is over 40 degrees F. This explains why that continuous seventy days and nights of frost in 1963 is memorable. Yet when it was over, and the rain came in March, it only took a couple of days to get used to mud instead of snow.

In recent years we have often had timely warning of cold from radio forecasts. Unfortunately they do not invariably seem able to predict a measure of intensity. In addition the danger of flooding can seldom be foretold. 'Heavy rain' is one thing, but four inches in four hours is a catastrophe anywhere, and the only time I was caught in it there was no warning.

The other fault in Met. weather forecasting is that they assume we all know the meaning of the words being used. This is certainly not the case, and a national farming paper published an article by Mr J. L. Jones on the subject in the winter of 1970. On the whole I think Wallace's Ground had taught me the difference between ground frost, air frost and wind frost. Ground frost is freezing at soil level, with the air a few feet higher well above 0 degrees C. It is usually fairly light, and occurs mainly on those still clear nights when the soil is losing heat fairly rapidly, but the cold air lies in a thin, undisturbed blanket. An air frost is often under similar still conditions, but when the blanket of air below 0 degrees C. is at least four feet thick. What we dread is a wind frost when all the air is well below 0 degrees C., and its movement enhances the influence of the low temperature.

I had no idea what causes the difference between black frost and hoar frost, until I read Mr Jones' article, but the names explain themselves for all practical purposes. In some ways it is surprising that the influence of all types of frost are most important when Wallace's Ground is growing crops. Cold may be very unpleasant for humans, but animals seem to be well protected against it. Their health is more likely to suffer in extremely wet weather. This applies to all forms of livestock including hens, but such a statement needs qualification.

Hens bred for the old systems of free range are like sheep in showing little harm from cold. At one time Wallace's Ground was used for another open air system of hen management, which was like free range in that the hens had cover, but no artificial heat, and were in direct contact with the soil. It was known as folding, and involved a light house with a wire pen attached. Each unit housed 25 hens and was moved every day to fresh grass. It meant even manuring of the soil, clean earth for the poultry, safety from foxes, and only small numbers being involved in any outbreak of disease. It was supplanted by intensive, indoor poultry keeping for two reasons. The daily moving of pens used much more labour than indoor husbandry, and a controlled environment could mean more eggs per bird, if the hens were bred for it.

It would seem to be proved beyond doubt that poultry bred for high yields indoors cannot stand the rigour of an outdoor winter. It is sometimes suggested that something similar has happened in breeding pigs for factory conditions indoors. Breeding sows were certainly similar to hens in being able to stand a great deal of cold in the fields, as long as they had some rough protection from rain and mud. The next query is what will happen to cows, which modern practice has already housed, even on dry land? With a final thought for the sheep, where housing is still unusual but is increasing fairly rapidly.

In the past the cold did not hurt any of the livestock kept on Wallace's Ground when it was in pasture. There was a slight danger of sheep being covered in drifting snow but they were near home, and easy to find. Frost on crops has always been a more serious danger, but the field was favoured to some extent by its position. There was also the fact that it never grew such risky crops as apples. These can be wiped out for the year by extreme cold at blossom time, whilst moderate frost can spoil the quality of the fruit.

The position of the field on a curving hill top saved it from being a frost pocket, which our garden was on the valley floor. Apparently in still conditions cold air flows like water into every hollow. This means that low, sheltered places may collect cold air, and suffer from frost. A good deal of modern work has been done on planting belts of trees at angles on slopes to deflect the flowing cold air from fertile valley fields. Wallace's Ground has no need for this, since its position protected it naturally.

Frost is doing rather more harm to ordinary farm crops than used to be the case. Potatoes were always a risk, and their position has not altered greatly. Real earlies are only grown in a few favoured areas such as Jersey, Cornwall,

Pembroke and Ayrshire. The main crop, however, will probably have produced leaves in May, and a late May frost can turn bright green foliage into a black abomination. Usually a second lot of shoots come up, but the crop is sadly reduced by the loss of the first growth. We were only potato growers under Government Orders during the war and just after, but I remember the next field to Wallace's Ground looking horrible as the result of one frost. This is unlikely to be seen again on the farm in my time. Since potatoes are now so highly mechanised the only way to make a profit would be to grow a big acreage. This would disrupt the present cropping system, and involve the purchase of a great deal of machinery. My nephew shows no sign of switching Wallace's Ground from more ordinary crops.

In saying that ordinary crops are a little more susceptible to frost damage than they once were, there is nothing very spectacular. Part of the change is due to varieties and rather more to management. Varieties of winter wheat have not lost hardiness. This crop is sown in October/November and has a strange habit of growth. The first grassy leaves come up and lie on the surface of the earth, sheltered by stones or clods. They then go through a resting period and only throw up erect, ear-bearing shoots in spring. The prostrate leaves are reasonably safe from cold, and if the plant does die out in an English winter it is much more likely to be due to waterlogged roots than to cold on the leaves. The peculiarity about winter wheat is that whenever it is sown it must go through a dormant stage. If a farmer has not been able to sow in autumn and has seed in hand, there is only a short period in early spring when true winter wheats can be used. By April a winter wheat will come up, go into a dormant stage, and then apparently decide not to send up any flowers or ears.

Spring wheats miss the prostrate, resting stage, and grow erect stems from the start. Generally their yield is lower than autumn wheats. The crop which is more open to frost damage than of old is oats. Winter oats have no prostrate resting stage, but the old variety 'Grey Winter' was very hardy. Newer types are much better croppers but these can all be damaged by hard frost. Oats flourish most in the wet west rather than in the colder, drier east. When frost has come to winter oats in Wallace's Ground they suffer, unless snow covered. Even with snow there are often patches where the wind has removed the cover.

With a vast reduction in horses there is less point in growing oats, so that frost damage on high-yielding winter varieties is no great worry.

Winter damage is much more important on grass grown as a crop, and the reasons for increased danger is the earliness of some varieties being sown, and the heavy use of nitrogen. In my youth mixtures of grasses and clovers were always grown. The controversy then was over the wisdom of sowing only three varieties of grasses and one clover, or trying to copy nature by using small quantities of a dozen to a score of grasses and clovers. Today it is likely that one very early grass will be sown and heavily fertilised. The aim is to get spring growth early and management involves dividing the field into 21 paddocks, grazed for one day only.

Even on the dry soil of Wallace's Ground there is a danger that cows will tread such small paddocks into a quagmire in late winter. In addition the very early grasses tend to grow straight up, and much more likely to be cut by frost than varieties which hug the ground. Finally the heavy use of fertiliser in previous years tends to make feeding easy for the plant. It grows a lot of leaf, but the roots have had no need to expand. Such poorly rooted grasses can be killed by the occasional season when we have weeks of real air frost.

In thinking about winter temperatures the important point to remember is that growth is determined more by the the warmth of the soil than of the air. In fact until mid-February in Wallace's Ground the sun has very little influence on the temperature of the air. Near the plant leaf level at least the air is warmed or cooled by the temperature of the soil. There is a different climate where herbage hugs the earth, than at our towering height of six foot above it. The soil stores heat, which is conducted down for several inches. The rate at which heat is absorbed or released depends to a large extent on soil moisture. A heavy clay holds moisture and there is less evaporation of water from the surface. A dry surface warms up quickly, which is one reason why a layer of straw on the surface will stop the earth freezing beneath it.

It takes a hard frost to get the earth frozen to a depth of four inches, and it is a matter of inches of soil which settle plant growth. Very seldom in Dorset do these few inches of frozen soil drop much below o degrees C., there is stored heat at lower levels to check really steep falls. This must be taken with the fact that bacteria can start work and plant growth is possible at just about 8 degrees C. of soil temperature. The amount of warming up required is very small, yet much of our farming is unconsciously directed towards it. The use of a mulch of straw has already been mentioned. Dung or compost would have a similar influence, and their effect on early growth is known to every farmer and gardener.

On the kindly soil of Wallace's Ground a similar aid to soil warming is to get the top few inches dry and fairly fine. This can be done by stirring the surface with tools in late winter and hoping for rainless days. On clay soils this is quite impossible, because wet clay cannot be stirred. Any tool will merely smear it to a surface quite impervious to water so that it may not dry for months, and then into something like bricks. Clay is best autumn ploughed and left in cocked-up furrows, hoping for a frost to crumble it without intervention by man.

To the countryman the lighter days at the end of January bring a curious lifting of the heart. The weather may be sterile with cold and snow until almost April, and it is quite likely that grass will not grow much until the end of March. Frequently fields are too waterlogged to cultivate, much less to sow. Yet the return of the sun is certain in the week before February. It may be that farmers have a sub-conscious memory of the days when winter could mean desperate starvation for man and beast. It is not long ago. My old Grandfather has told me of winters when the cows were too weak to walk to the first pasture of spring. They had to be hauled from the sheds by horses or plough oxen which had the first priority on the farm store of food.

Well within my own memory there were winter shortages, even in farmhouse fare. We did not expect any fresh eggs, and had to be content with what my Mother had preserved in 'water glass'. This was a solution of silicate of soda. From memory it was supposed to seal the shell of an egg, which is normally porous. This kept out air and slowed the decay of the contents. We did not eat boiled water-glass eggs, but they were tolerable scrambled, and satisfactory for cake making. Then, although I do not remember being without milk in tea, there was never enough to make into butter in autumn, and it was an extremely variable substance.

The winter feeding of animals had not reached its present level in my boyhood. Hens were given inferior grain and no purchased source of protein such as fish meal. Indeed plenty of townsmen still use the term 'chick feed' for something inferior and cheap. It is about the last thing in the world a modern poultry farmer would give to his hens.

There is something ironic about the fact that when we really needed preserved foods in winter there were no methods of providing a satisfactory product. Today, when there is not the slightest difficulty in producing an abundance of fresh eggs and milk at any season 'convenience' foods are in every shop. Canned new potatoes, frozen broad beans, long-life milk and freeze-dried peas are very nearly as good as fresh. The dread of winter hunger has gone from man and beast, but it is still very good to be able to say 'The days are really giving out.' Nothing can stop the coming of spring.

Chapter Three

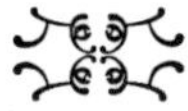

Awakening

Some calendars give the Vernal Equinox, March 21st, as the first day of spring. My own preference is for Lady Day, March 25th, which is when quarterly bills become due. Paying bills acts as a damper on feelings of excitement and joy, which the season would normally produce. It is in keeping that there should be a check because every English spring has set-backs, when winter seems to have returned. The general picture is of a first slow stirring, followed by a breathless rush of change in the crops and hedges of Wallace's Ground. It is impossible to take it all in when there is something new every day. The grey rainy days can be almost a relief. They do not halt the awakening, but there is less danger of too much beauty being overwhelming.

The first realisation of returning light comes to me in the last week of January. This is still mid-winter according to the calendar, and there are few very noticeable signs of spring in the mildest weather. The buds on shrubs and trees are far from opening, but they are swelling slightly and pointing upward in a way that was far less noticeable in December. The robins protect their territories by short bursts of song throughout the entire winter. They start by leading a completely solitary life, but by the end of January they may have paired, although not mated. The Field is surrounded by hedges, but on one of the longer sides there is a lane. This means that an amount of cover is available from two hedges close together. Here the robins need a shorter length of fence as a living space.

Even in late spring there is not a great deal of bird song from the hedges. Modern machinery has kept the shrubs too short for birds. The wren is almost alone in liking the dense growth produced by annual trimming. In January they crowd three or four together in last year's nest. Blackbirds show a distinct preference for the village gardens, where their winter needs are helped by scraps thrown out for them. In a long spell of mild weather, starting in late January, it is not unusual to find them in full song. Usually only one pair of thrushes come to Wallace's Ground. There are three trees in the lane hedge which provides a high place for song, but most of the present hedges are too short for them, and dry land is none too good for slugs and snails in spring. The thrush will give his full spring song as early as December, and only stops in bitter weather. I have a fancy that his outpouring is even better in the dusk than just before sunrise. Possibly this is no more than a feeling of personal thanksgiving that the day's work is over.

Of all the music of the little hills the song of the skylark is possibly the best, and spread over most hours of the day. He also sings for at least seven months of the year. In late spring I have heard larks long after dark, or long before dawn. It is difficult to be sure how to classify 2 a.m. which is what most of us regard as nightingale time. I fear that larks are less abundant than they used to be over Wallace's Ground, but not by any means extinct. The usual height for the male to hover and to sing is about 100 feet. It is very pleasant to find the song continuing as he slowly drops to the ground. It has been suggested that the pre-dawn and after dusk singing of the lark is because at 100 feet he is in sunlight when the earth is dark. This only gives a few minutes of extra time, and certainly does not account for the 2 a.m. song I have quoted.

The birds of Wallace's Ground change considerably with the season, and I am not thinking of migrants such as cuckoos and swallows. The peewit – often called lapwing or plover – nests on the hills, but spends the winter in flocks, seeking unfrozen land near valley streams. The flocking instincts varies enormously with different birds. We have seen that the robin is completely solitary for several months, whilst the blackbirds are in pairs. The rook could be said to flock all the year since even at nesting time they gather in close companionship. Against this the bullfinches forage in flocks along the hedges in winter, but separate into pairs for nesting. The chaffinch and the greenfinch search the ground and the hedge ditch for seeds, in a very mixed company. In a sunny February they may separate into pairs or family groups and change the chirping of winter for real song. Rather strangely they will revert to flocks if the weather turns hard, and nest building is unlikely before early April. The goldfinch is sometimes an autumn visitor after they have flocked, but I have never found a nest in the Field. This is a pity because their mating song is very sweet, and their plumage is true gold. The autumn visits are less frequent than they were in my boyhood, when the Field was in permanent pasture, and they came to flutter round seeding thistles. Modern farming does not allow clumps of thistles.

Some of the opponents of weed killers imply that these chemicals are the sole reason why bird life has changed, and some butterflies are becoming rare. This is a gross exaggeration, and poisoning by sprays is possibly not even the main reason. Very often it is efficient cultivation which has removed the wild creatures' food supply. For instance, in Wallace's Ground it has been cultivation which has wiped out the seeding thistles for the finches, and banished the stinging nettles beloved by some butterflies. On nearby downland there was a turf which was at least a hundred years old, plus some slopes which had never been cultivated. The turf was utterly different from the plants grown today, and had its own blue butterfly. If man grows a crop every other species of plant is a weed, and all his cultivations are aimed at killing competitors for his crop. Even if the down is restored to pasture for a few years, every effort is made to grow less than half-a-dozen kinds of grass and clover.

The herbage of the old down had hundreds of different plants, some agriculturally useless, such as dwarf thistles, many reasonably nutritious although not very productive, and not a few extremely pleasant to see and to smell. Of the latter the wild thyme comes to mind immediately, and this is eaten by sheep. The ploughing of the downs has not only removed the food plants of birds and butterflies, but has interfered with breeding. The peewit, the lark and the partridge make their nests on the soil. Cultivation is an obvious danger, but damage is almost more likely in the management of temporary pasture. The grasses are bred to be ready for harvest very early, and are fertilised to make this even earlier. What is worse is that grass is often conserved as silage rather than hay, which means cutting before a flower stem is formed. All these things added together may mean the mower arrives in early May instead of mid-June, and there is no hope of escape.

A nest in a field of corn may well be empty by harvest, and this is where the peewits are likely to nest. The larks liked the old down turf, but they too can survive except when Wallace's Ground is in cultivated grass. Partridges were never very common in the Field, or anywhere on the farm. The reason used to be that for centuries the landlord was Winchester College, who were not interested in game. Most squires did not allow their tenants to shoot anything except rabbits, and rabbits would have been banned if a bit of Agricultural Law had not made their destruction a joint right held by landlord and tenant. A parish in which every little farmer can kill partridges and peasants is bound to mean these birds will be scarce, especially since no one is breeding any, or controlling predators.

On farms in other parts of the chalk uplands partridges are barely holding their own, even with good keepering. Strips of rough grazing must be provided between crops, and keepers must locate and mark nests so that mowing machines may avoid them. This with artificial rearing, and the control of foxes may save the partridge from extinction.

I can remember only one nest in Wallace's Ground, and that is 40 years ago. It was in a disused cart track in a shallow rut. The young were hatched but none reached maturity, in spite of the most wonderful devotion by both parents. Their loss was entirely from predators, and convinced me that the old keepers were not far wrong in killing a wide range of birds and beasts who have a liking for partridges.

In modern days country-lovers tend to aim at conserving all wild life, and give convincing figures about diet to show that game predators are harmless. This is perfectly true if game birds are really wild, and thin on the ground. The shooting man wants them very unnaturally thick on the ground, much as the farmer aims at a crop of, say, barley containing no other plant. In country sport adjacent landlords have usually tried to be neighbourly. The keen shooting man wants the hunt to find a fox when they meet on his estate, although he knows what a fox can do to his semi-tame birds. Early on the morning of the meet the keeper goes to a trusted neighbour, and digs out a good fox, which is placed in a bag. This fox is released in a small coppice, or field of kale, well after daylight, when he is unlikely to move out of cover. The Master of Hounds solemnly asks the keeper for advice at the meet, and surprisingly a fox is always found. For the rest of the winter any fox on a shooting estate very soon becomes a skin, and this is one of the perks of the keeper.

Wallace's Ground never had a fox burrow in my memory, but we had stoats, weasels, and rats in the hedges, plus sparrow hawks, magpies and jays in the air. None of these have been controlled, but one old shepherd was a master at trapping roving foxes. I know he had eight in one winter, which paid him nicely in pelts. His main reason was that foxes can do terrible things to sheep, especially in taking the the first born of a twin, whilst the second is being born. Shep got a bonus on twins, and in any case had a genuine affection for his sheep.

The hedges of Wallace's Ground are trimmed every year by machine, but across the lane on the north side is a field farmed by a neighbour and here the hedge has been treated less harshly. It is not overgrown by any means as many hedges were in the bad days between the wars. At most the growth is three years old, whereas before machine trimming a good farmer had his hedges laid about every eight years. There is a big difference, though, between annual trimming, and only three years growth.

In February the uncut hedge has some six feet long,

straggling, blackberry stems, the growth of last year. These already carry a very few young green leaves, which will blacken and die if winter returns. A more beautiful sign of spring is the yellow catkins on the hazel bushes. These are the male flowers and produce vast quantities of pollen. The female flower is tiny and inconspicuous. If it is to be fertilised to form a nut the pollen must drift to it on the air, which is the reason why the male catkins are so numerous. The normal height of a hazel bush is 10 to 15 feet, and if it is shorn every year no catkins are produced. It will be strange never to see them again in Wallace's Ground, nor to keep an eye on the hedge in autumn for ripe nuts. I hope the neighbour across the lane will continue to let his hedge grow a little taller than is the present fashion.

The straight hedges and the rectangular shape of the field make it almost certain that the land was fenced about 150 years ago, when the Common land of the village was enclosed. Old paddocks are usually smaller, with fences which follow the contour of the land, or border a winding brook, or mark a sudden change of soil. Wallace's Field had no great difference in slope, no drain, and no soil variation. The hedges were planted as fences, and to mark the boundary of a holding.

There were two things to be considered, first that the fence should be stockproof, and second that the shrubs should have a value. This was not easy to combine and in many districts it has not been attempted. The blackthorn and the hawthorn make the best stockproof fences, but their trimmings are useless. Hazel and ash cut every 8 to 10 years will yield wood for farm hurdles, and poles for hay cribs. Tall timber trees in a hedge have a timber value, but the shrubs in their shade grow weakly and allow livestock to escape. In the Midlands many hedges are of pure thorn. In Dorset vales there are many trees in the fences, but originally Wallace's Ground had a mixture of thorn, hazel and ash.

Hedging was a skilled winter job, the essence of which was that every 8 to 10 years the shrubs were cut to ground level, and could renew themselves from new growth. Obviously this would leave three or four years with no stockproof fence, so there had to be a variation. A few branches were cut nearly through at ground level but not quite. They were then bent over and pegged down to make a barrier. These partially severed branches stayed alive, but the new growth came from completely severed shoots, and from their own roots; these grew up through the 'laid' barrier.

I used the term 'lay' for this form of hedging, but some districts call it 'pleaching'. The bent over branches were fastened in place by 'binders', which were long shoots woven around the top of stakes. 'Heathering' has the same meaning as binding, and the stakes are dead wood in Dorset but live branches in some other counties. The whole process varies in detail, but the essence is a fence of laid branches, which will be completely removed when the hedge is made again in eight year's time, plus the fact that the growth is always new wood from soil level.

The coming of the mechanical hedge cutter means annual trimming but no cutting back to ground level. New wood is continually removed with the main shrub getting older without renewal from the base. The thorns stand this very well and may last indefinitely. Ash and hazel are not so happy. The annual trimming at three to four feet makes a bushy top, but old main stems tend to die, and holes appear in the bottom of the hedge. Possibly a stretch of hedge containing mainly ash and hazel might no longer be a fence in a score of years. There are signs of this in Wallace's Ground. In addition the annual shearing has an influence on other plants in the hedge.

It must be remembered that new enclosures, such as Wallace's Ground, are 150 years old. Many plants are found in the hedges which were certainly not planted. Probably some came in as seeds from berries eaten by birds. This is probably true of holly, of which there is only one bush in the field. Holly can make a very attractive fence, as many gardeners know, but I do not think it was planted in many farm fences. Perhaps gardeners are not superstitious because they do much trimming of their holly bushes, whereas hedgers know it is unlucky to cut it. I have seen machine operators take a lot of trouble to avoid a bush. Cutting is only allowed to get a few berried branches on Christmas Eve.

Another shrub sown by birds is elder. This was kept in gardens because fruit and flower could be used in a number of medicines, ointments and wines. It is quite useless in a fence because it smothers other bushes, and is very brittle. It is badly influenced by annual trimming, and quickly leads to gaps at well under my estimate for hazel of a score of years.

Brambles were almost certainly spread by birds, and if anything they are improved by annual trimming. They make shorter, denser, shoots which blend with the hedge and repel livestock. Bryony sprawls over hedges and has no value as a fence. Its berries are poisonous and dangerous for children, but I have never known animals eat it. The hedge trimmer does not seem to have altered it much in Wallace's Ground, and I confess to a liking for the look of those bright green fruits which ripen to scarlet. Honeysuckle is another useless climbing herb, but has no poisonous drawbacks, and a wonderful scent. It has just survived the trimmer, but has been much reduced where the hedge is very short.

Before the close annual cutting by machinery there were a few crab apples in one of the hedges. These may have been sown by birds, but it is equally likely that there were a few planted by men, since they were commonly used in country cooking. My Mother made some wonderful crab apple jelly. By whatever method the crabs first reached the hedge it is fairly certain that the originals did not survive for 150 years. The old hedger left them as he did the holly, so they became fairly tall trees. With no renewal from ground level a life of a century and a half is unlikely. In addition my memory of them is not of obvious, knarled age. The crab apples I reached for Mother were on vigorious growth. Almost certainly they grew naturally from seed during the present century, and the mechanisation of the last decade has wiped them out.

Another shrub which has not taken very kindly to annual cutting is the spindle tree, but it has survived. The flowers are not very noticeable, and will not open until late spring, but in autumn the bright red berries are magnificent. This was probably not planted but was introduced by birds. The leaves and twigs are poisonous. Apart from this a spindle bush in a hedge had an attraction for gipsies who were not welcome visitors in the lane. They had a use for the wood which could make the 'skewers' which butchers used to employ in holding a rolled rib of beef in place. It was also good for clothes pegs, and for rather primitive knitting needles. All these uses have gone but old countrymen still talk of the spindle tree as 'skewer wood'. Incidentally I am unable to explain why scientists refer to it as the spindle 'tree'; it is a shrub which seldom grows more than eight feet tall, and is more often under five feet.

There is a stronger reason for destroying spindle trees than the fact that we no longer use wooden skewers, or that it has caused poisoning. The poisoning is unlikely to happen anyway because like most toxic plants it has an unpleasant taste. It is a curse because of connection with broad beans. Every gardener has seen his broad beans invaded by the 'black army'. These are black aphids which smother the growing tips and the flowers, so that a crop can be completely destroyed. They appear on beans in summer but spend the winter as eggs on spindle trees. They are laid in autumn near buds and hatch at the first sign of spring in February. They develop slowly at first but may cause the curling of spindle leaves in April. A winged form develops, and these fly to broad beans. When beans are grown on a field scale the aphids always spread in from the edge of the field.

Beans have never been grown in Wallace's Ground in my time. They flourish on more clayey soils, but the aphids from its hedges could well reach the gardens of the village. It takes only a fortnight in May for one winged female to produce 1,000 individuals on your bean tips. This knowledge has been available for much of my life, and it seems strange that no determined effort has been made to wipe out the spindle tree. The aphid can winter on a few other plants such as the Guelder Rose, but the spindle tree is its favourite host. Possibly it escaped because beans are not grown as a field crop on large stretches of the lighter soils of the country, and the gardener can protect his beans by spraying without much difficulty. I like the look of the autumn berries, and the odd bush in the hedges of Wallace's Ground has never influenced farm profits.

One hedgerow plant appears to escape all damage from annual, close trimming. The wild clematis – 'Old Man's Beard' – is an unmitigated curse to the hedge as a fence. Some people call it 'Traveller's Joy', and both these common names give the impression that it is a pleasant herb. I suppose it is beautiful on someone else's hedge, when the fruits hang down in autumn as a white, dense mass, like a huge, white, silky beard.

All parts of the climbing, sprawling plant are highly poisonous, but once more very unpalatable. I have seen sheep nibble at it but immediately spit it out. The booklet on 'British Poisonous Plants' states that it causes severe irritation in the mouths of animals. The old hedgers cut it out when they laid a hedge, once in eight years. This did very little to check it, but the new hedging machine does even less. Cutting it back to the same level as the rest of the hedge merely stimulates growth, and fantastically rapid growth is what makes clematis a curse. It literally smothers every shrub. Wallace's Ground hedges are relatively free from it, but in neighbouring fields on the farm it has slowly destroyed the fences. One hedge was bulldozed because it no longer had any purpose, except as a support for Traveller's Joy.

This bulldozing is memorable for me because very little hedge removal has taken place on the farm. Many people are greatly concerned that the landscape in many districts is being altered by the removal of hedges. In my native fields one hedge was removed because clematis had made it useless. In Putt Ground, west of Wallace's Ground, a hedge was uprooted on one side of a lane because the lane no longer had a purpose. It led to a field which was rented by another farmer until 1909, when my Father took it over.

The only other grubbing was of a one acre plot, which had once been the pasture for the horse of a village tradesman. The Germans started the clearing in 1940 by dropping a land mine on the hedge. We wanted to plough the lot, and a one acre field is a nuisance for modern machines. In any case it would have cost almost as much to make good the German damage as to take out the rest of the hedge.

The fences of Wallace's Ground will stay since a 13 acre field is no great nuisance to machines. On the rest of the farm of 600 acres the average field size is a bit larger, probably about 20 acres, and there is one field of 43 acres and another of 32 acres. These will remain unless the close trimming of hedges does destroy them, and complete destruction is unlikely. My nephew is more likely to be faced with hedges which are no longer stockproof, but which now occupy very little room, and would cost a lot to uproot, rather like roadside hedges in East Anglia.

On a farm devoted entirely to crops it would be true that a 13 acre field wastes time, because machines have to turn at the boundaries, when it would be more efficient to give them a longer uninterrupted run. Wallace's Ground is part of a farm which keeps sheep and cattle, as well as growing crops, so that fences are necessary. The only essential break with the past is that the gates in common use should be wide enough to let implements through without any difficulty. Many of our wide machines can be packed up for the few occasions when they have to go on the public roads, but this waste of time must be avoided for passing between fields.

Not only are the vast majority of the fields of the size they have been for a century, but there has been an increase in fences in the last dozen years. No new hedges have been planted, but at least seven of the new fences are semi-permanent. One occurs in Wallace's Ground where no effort has been made to remove the wire fence which was put up when the Parish Council took part of the Ground as a playing field. This 5 to 6 acres is back in normal farming, but the fence has its uses when the field is used for livestock. In addition the big 43 acre field is wire fenced into three parts, and the 32 acre in two parts. These are substantial wire fences with gates, and are obviously part of my nephew's plan of farming. They do not provide shelter, but presumably are useful in controlling grazing when their turn comes for a break from corn crops.

This is not what some people have described as 'paddock grazing'; all the enclosures are much too big. When the cattle are grazing they are confined in much smaller paddocks, made by an electric fence, which is moved every day. These semi-permanent wire fences seem strange to some people in a countryside where fields might have been expected to get bigger. The one in Wallace's Ground is exceptional. It might have been left because the Parish Council made a substantial job of erecting it, and it would cost a bit to remove. This is not true of the fixed wire in Horse Ground, the Big Down, Bellamy's Down, and at Pat's Castle. This is all connected with stock farming, and its rotational use of the land.

On this farm Conservationists need not fear an end to the patchwork pattern of the landscape. Hedges will not be uprooted, but three cider orchards are gone, and trees are unlikely to be replaced. There never were any trees in Wallace's Ground. On the other side of the lane three decrepit ash trees survive of what used to be a skyline row of a score. I remember one being struck by lightning, and the whole trunk was split from the top to the root underground. The strength of such a blow still fills me with awe. On the main road in the valley one ivy-clad decaying elm survives from a row of five, which were once magnificent towering giants. On the hill top a few trees remain of the clump which sheltered Pat's Castle. All are past their prime and have outlived both usefulness and timber value. This was never tree country, and most planting was for cider, or game cover, or deliberate landscaping. Trees are not natural but the spring shades of dozens of crops in fields will last my time.

The hedges of Wallace's Ground never produced anything very popular in the way of spring flowers on their banks. There were no primroses and no bluebells. On south facing banks celandines open in the noon sunshine as early as February, but celandines are no use as picked flowers to take home. On the far side of the southern hedge there used to be a few yards of fragrant white violets. I have not seen them lately. The annual trimming keeps the hedge very narrow, and this makes it possible to plough much closer to the bushes. This means that the bank is much narrower than it used to be, which has impaired some of its beauty as well as reducing its influence as a nuisance. The old wide banks grew docks, tall thistles and weed grasses, all of which tended to creep out into the field. There was also a patch of charming herbs with flowers like potato flowers in shape, but with a yellow centre and purple petals. In Autumn it produces bright red berries.

We always called this plant 'nightshade' and for many years I thought it was the terrible Deadly Nightshade. Actually the two flowers are not a bit alike, but it may have been just as well that children should have a fear of the 'nightshade' of Wallace's Ground. It is quite poisonous enough to cause serious illness if those pretty red berries are eaten, and children sometimes seem to have little sense of taste. Possibly their taste is perfectly good and their danger lies in a juvenile bit of gluttony, which leads to picking a large handful before their playmates, and cramming the mouth very full. The other common name for our nightshade is 'Bitter Sweet', which is no real deterrent, since bittersweet apples are better than no apples. Animals have the sense to avoid this hedgerow pest.

In a way it is a bit remarkable that cows have never taken enough nightshade to hurt them from this hedge. They are far less selective in their grazing than sheep. Their tongue takes a wide sweep round a clump of herbage and the whole lot is swallowed. Sheep can pick daintily at the individual plants they fancy. Against this sheep show a much greater liking than cattle for hedgerow plants. Possibly sheep on the ploughable soils are confined much more to a monotonous diet such as kale or a cultivated ley containing no variety of grasses and herbs. Certainly the sheep coming to Wallace's Ground from, say, turnips tend to make straight for the hedge bank.

The first thing they eat is often the ivy, but they also like plaintains and yarrow. Many old shepherds refer to ivy as 'sheep's medicine', and my Mother used an infusion of the leaves to take the shine from worn serge suits. Of the latter use I can only say that the shine soon returned, but in 1970

I was told she should have used the black ivy berries! As to the 'sheep's medicine', this may be less of an old wive's tale. Many medicines in excess are poisons, and there have been causes when illness has followed wild indulgence on ivy. A. A. Forsyth reports distress in cattle who had access to a large clump of wilted ivy which had been stripped from a house. I have never known sheep the worse or the better for cropping the ivy on the hedge banks of Wallace's Ground.

The first scent of spring is from the white violets on the far side of the south hedge. This can be expected in late February unless we get one of those unusual winters which drag on to the end of March. Almost every year there will be a day with some warmth in the sun before March 1st, and noon is the best time to stoop over any small remaining clump in the bank. White violets are much less common with us than the pale dog violet, which has very little scent. Some botanists class the white violet with the dark, bluish-purple 'viola odorata'. They both have a much stronger scent than the dog violet, but nothing approaching the perfume of some of the cultivated forms.

When Wallace's Ground is ploughed it is not unusual to have another plant of the violet family as an annual weed in crops. The wild pansy has nothing much in the way of scent, it does little damage, and the flowers are small. I mention it because the common name is Heartsease. Another wild perennial flower, nearer to the colour and size of the garden pansy can be found in mountain pastures, but not on the little hills of Dorset.

To me the real beginning of the obvious up-surge of returning life is in the scent of primroses. It was very fitting that village churches used to be largely decorated with tight bunches of primroses on Easter Sunday. They convey more about the Resurrection than the sophisticated 'floral art' of today, although I hope the decorators in my home church will not think their efforts are being scorned. Primroses go with Easter, holly with Christmas and enormous vegetable marrows with Harvest Festival.

In my youth, when Wallace's Ground had been in pasture for a half century, there were some plants of the primrose family in the field. Now it is necessary to wander a few hundred yards to find any. The cowslips open in late April, and so do the more luxuriant oxlips. Both have a delicate scent very similar to the primrose, and there used to be quite a few cowslips in the Field, before it was ploughed. Oxslips are found on better, more moist valley soils, and primroses in hedge banks or in coppices.

It has always seemed strange that the botanists who could name the delicately scented violets *Viola odorata* could think of nothing better for primroses than *Primula vulgaris*. To be fair 'vulgar' has changed its meaning. It used to mean no more than 'familiar'. The English Book of Common Prayer is in the 'vulgar tongue'.

The first flowers of spring are usually white, or yellow, or blue. In a strange way they give a feeling of youth, very different from the mature, flamboyant colours of autumn. In Wallace's Ground the first extensive blooming is in the hedges, where the blackthorn opens its small white blossoms in March, before the leaves appear. The fruit of the blackthorn is the sloe, and there is a tradition that there will be a cold spell when the blackthorn is in flower. These 'blackthorn winters' are fairly sure to happen, since the thorn is in flower for several weeks in late March and April. It is easy to get a reputation for weather lore at this season by waiting for the cold which is almost sure to return briefly, and then pointing to the flowers in the hedge.

Another thorn in the Field is the Hawthorn, May, Quick or Whitethorn. This again has white flowers, but they do not appear before May or early June. Rather curiously every one of the common names quoted has a meaning. The fruit is a 'haw' which is a red berry of the rose family. It flowers in May, and 'quick' is a reference to the remarkable speed of growth to form a prickly barrier. Whitethorn is a reference to the colour of the scented flowers. It is sometimes claimed to be the best hedging plant on the farm, although the blackthorn runs it very close. It certainly stands hard annual trimming by hedging machines, but this means far less blossom. The world will be poorer if no hawthorn hedge is ever neglected, and we never travel for miles along a road with walls of white bloom on either hand. This is especially magical on a still evening in June, after a warm day, when the scent is at its best. This fragrance has nothing heavy or drowsy about it. Like the white blossom it is the essence of youth, energy, and hope.

In Wallace's Ground there will remain some May blossom, but not the abundance which flourished when the hedges were not cut more often than every eighth year. There will be some haws for the birds, and the blackthorn will yield enough fruit for sloe gin. Most recipes for this cordial seem to contain much more gin than sloes.

It is a little unexpected to find how many plants in the hedges are of the rose family, both useful and as hedge weeds. The whitethorn and blackthorn were planted, and possibly the crab apple. The blackberry, or bramble, is a nuisance in a fence, but most of us enjoy the fruit. The devil spits on the berries on Michaelmas Day and they should not be eaten after this. Actually they do tend to become mildewed and past their best, rather suddenly, about the end of September.

Of the wild roses Wallace's Ground has two, both of which are pleasant, but not useful as fencing plants. The sweet briar foliage has a delicate, aromatic scent, which is only pronounced if the plant is bruised. The dog rose flower is sweet scented, and opens late in spring. This briar survives annual trimming, but there is now very little blossom on our side of the lane because the flowers come on second year growth. Probably the heavy trimming is responsible for the loss of the one wild cherry, which grew about eight feet high, and whose white flowers came a little earlier in spring than the crab apples.

As I have said, spring comes to Wallace's Ground at its earliest in the hedgerows with the pointing of buds, and the first flowers of hazel catkins. The commercial, farming surface varies much more with the weather, and the type of cropping. It is no exaggeration to claim that growth can be as early as February or as late as mid-April, but these dates are both unusual. Autumn sown wheat is beginning to look thicker and greener in most seasons by the end of February, but has not yet produced any erect stems to carry the flowers of grain. This is the time when nitrogenous fertilisers will be applied to stimulate growth. It is also the time when similar manures will be broadcast if the field is in grass. The hope is for early growth for grazing, or a heavier cut for hay. Similarly, if the field is to be sown to barley or oats it is desirable to get the seed in the earth by early March. A fertiliser containing the three main plant foods will be sown in the same row with the seed, and lightly raked over by a harrow.

Normally for spring sowing the land is ploughed in the autumn and the furrows left to be soaked with winter rain, and frozen by frost. The surface fades to a dead grey, with a few patches of dirty white, and a litter of flints. Immediately before the seed is sown this soil must be raked over to level it, and to make the earth into the crumb structure suitable for a seed bed. A minimum of stirring is desirable at this time of the year, because a dry spell is possible, and in any case once the crop starts growing it will remove an enormous amount of water from the surface. Most of us find it difficult to believe that in our English climate there is hardly a year when a field like Wallace's Ground would not pay for irrigation. This applies to grass as well as to all crops, but in saying it would pay I am assuming we could pump water from a river or store without paying any form of water rate. Our forefathers knew nothing about irrigation with sprinklers, but they did appreciate that excessive spring cultivations could be dangerous in drying the top few inches of soil.

The first pass of the harrows on this land which has stayed unmoved and grey for the winter is startling. The earth shows as a deep brown with more than a tinge of red in it, and it looks fertile. The seed drills follow, and before the rich colour fades again it is replaced by the wonderful new green of the cereal seedlings. Then comes the tall growth of high summer, and the ripe tints of autumn. Only on ploughed land in mid-winter does the soil look dead.

The rich living look of the soil after spring stirring and sowing is peculiar to the season. Autumn ploughing changes a dead stubble to brown earth, but there is something lacking in the look of freshly moved soil in the fall. Probably it is a combination of feelings produced by all the senses, and helped by conscious thought. It may seem a curious use of words to say that the colour of the earth of Wallace's Ground after spring harrowing gives a feeling of urgency. Perhaps it is no more than the energetic scent of spring, plus the pleasant warmth of the sun in the shelter of the hedge, and the unusual noise in this quiet place of tractors labouring at their top speed. Reasoning comes into it because speed in getting the seed into the land is obviously desirable.

A great deal of farm work is routine, especially in the care of livestock. It is desirable to stick to a timetable, but an extra half hour at market or watching hounds is not crucial for the profits of the year. On very wet, sticky clay ploughing before Christmas may be extremely important, because the passage of a tractor may become impossible after heavy rain and for months at a time afterwards, yet the job feels boring. Wallace's Ground presents no such winter problem. Once the rain stops, the snow melts, or the frost thaws we know we can get on with ploughing from September to February. There is no need for overtime or for anxiety. The spring sowing is different. Even on this kindly soil we have to wait, until the raking action of the harrows will make a pleasant, even seedbed – a layer of crumbs of soil, neither in clods nor a dry powder. This layer can easily become much too dry, or run together in the rain to form a curiously impervious surface. Seedtime is urgent, and every hour of daylight must be used. There is excitement in finishing the job before darkness.

The tractors do not weary, but they share one fault with the old horses. Pushing them hard in spring may lead to breakdowns in health. There is small comfort in realising that a breakdown in the tractor health is usually due to negligence in servicing, whereas with no one at fault a horse was liable to be in poor condition in spring after a winter without grass. Influenza was fairly common in horses just when they were most needed, and carters always over-serviced them, if grossly over-feeding can be compared with tractor lubrication.

The 'litter of flints' I mentioned are even more of a problem than they used to be. In Wallace's Ground they are not very large – mainly sharply angular knobs about four inches by two inches. Many have very sharp edges and it would be very easy to believe that some had been chipped by Stoneage men to form axes, or spear heads. Indeed this could be true, since there are many relics from pre-history on our chalk uplands. Generally speaking, however, the skilled men who shaped the flints worked in places where these stones were more abundant, and they left behind large quantities of chippings.

In Wallace's Ground the flints are mixed sparingly with the soil. In the adjoining Beck's Bottom they form an almost unbroken covering after the soil has been cultivated, and some are fairly massive and unbroken, say, one foot by four inches. It looks as if no crop could possibly grow through it, but the soil is not barren by any means. The trouble is that flints are hard on plough shares, on all cultivating machines, on any type of mower, and on tractor tyres. Their presence often makes an unwanted passage by tractors a necessity. On non-flinty soils rollers are used to crack knobs, and to firm some types of puffy land. On the chalk it may be necessary to use a very heavy roller as the last operation, to push the stones down out of the way of mowers and combine harvesters.

At this stage I would digress to explain my first understanding of the flints which are so important in the Field. For much of my life the village has been owned by Winchester College, and under their rule there was about an acre of unfenced land in the valley, just where the lane starts to climb steeply to Wallace's Ground. Here the chalk hill had been cut back by generations of villagers to form a cliff face. The chalk was not used for spreading on the soil as an improver. The plough fields were on the hill top, and it was cheaper to dig conical pits in each field. As far as I remember no one paid anything for chalk from the village hill face. It was used in small quantities to make rammed floors in old buildings and had been an ingredient in the cobb walls of cottages and barns. My memory of it was for whitening hearths in farm houses as a contrast to the large, black, polished, cooking stoves.

On the top of the bare cliff face there was a patch of turf on which old Lizzie Riggs had erected poles and clothes lines. She was the recognised village washer-woman, and used to toil up the hill with heavy baskets when she was well over seventy. I doubt if anyone charged her for the use of this airy drying ground, but I remember moving some posts in November because this was also the site for the village bonfire. On the flat below the chalk cliffs was the village pound where straying animals could be held. Next to it was a sawpit, which presumably paid no rent. This was an old device for turning tree trunks into planks. It was used by the wagon builder and his mate. Their saw had a handle at each end and one man was in the pit, with his mate on the surface, enjoying much more comfort as 'top sawyer'.

All these relics from the old days have vanished. Since Winchester College sold the village there have been several changes of ownership, less in complete farms, but in odd houses and in plots of land. The approach to the lane leading to Wallace's Ground is quite unrecognisable. Lizzie's old drying plot and the chalk pit have been bulldozed to make a garden, with tomato houses where once was a sawpit. The village pound has vanished and been replaced by motor sheds. It is no longer possible to see a clean chalk cliff which would tell the story of the soil of Wallace's Ground.

On the top there was about six inches of soil. All the rest of the face was chalk, with veins of flint stones, each vein about four inches thick, and with some three feet of chalk between them.

In the long ages when frost, rain and vegetation formed that layer of soil, the weathering of the surface came mainly from chalk and not from the flint. The chalk is soft stuff, and crumbles readily on freezing. Worms move easily through it, mixing in rotting vegetation to make the dark material we know as mould. As this process went very slowly downwards, the thin bands of flint stones were reached, and these were untouched by rain or frost or earthworms. When men stirred the surface to grow a crop they mixed the flints with the soil. Much of the stirring by ploughs and harrows tended to bring the flints to the surface. In fact almost every form of cultivation lifts and shakes the soil, which is equivalent to sieving the stones to the top.

Motor transport was not widely used before the 1914–18 war, but road making for horse-drawn vehicles had been greatly improved by the eighteenth century. Hundreds of toll houses go back to that time, and were still in use in my Grandfather's day. Tolls went to private companies called Turnpike Trusts, and Grandfather told me how they crossed fields to avoid the Gates on their way to Dorchester Market. Most tolls were abolished after 1895, when the County Councils took over main roads, but for many years afterwards road making and repairing had to rely on local materials. On the chalk our only stone was flint, whilst ten miles to the south they used gravel from the heath, and ten miles north they quarried limestone.

Wallace's Ground and every other cultivated field on the chalk had a super-abundance of flints, and the lowliest form of farm labour for children was picking stones into heaps, which were carted to the side of the lane. For grown men an equally low status-job was cracking flints to a size demanded by road surveyors. It was badly paid but quite skilled. I have tried it in the lane outside the Ground, and never discovered just how or where to tap a stone to make it fracture. Not that I wanted to learn. It is a tiring job, and it was necessary to wear wire spectacles all day, to save the eyes from flying splinters.

We certainly had far too many stones, especially in the field adjoining Wallace's Ground, and we regarded it as a necessity to get them picked. There was a belief that they must be picked and not raked off, because raking removed too many. A thin covering was supposed to protect the soil from the hot sun of June. Personally I have no faith in this tradition. Our trouble was that all our neighbours had flints to sell, and the road surveyor was suspected of favouring farmers who were members of the Council, especially if they were on the Highway Committee.

In spite of not being on the Council my Father usually

managed to get something for his flints, until the whole demand collapsed with the coming of motors, leading to ease in getting better road-making stone from a distance. Since then no flints have been raked or picked, and yet for some reason they are no more a nuisance than they were in my youth. We certainly have much heavier rollers for pushing them underground, but against this the soil is now stirred to a greater depth, which might have been expected to increase the flints on the surface. It seems strange that flints do not appear to have increased after a half century without picking. Perhaps it is equally peculiar that a couple of hundred years of autumn picking left them still abundant.

It is impossible to think of springtime in Wallace's Ground without some reference to Easter. The passage of the years has changed thoughts and feelings about holidays and holy days. In boyhood one of my jobs was to drive the heifers in the Field down to the stream in the valley for a drink. On Good Fridays I did this soon after breakfast because by 10 a.m., or thereabouts, the village baker would be driving his van up the village with real hot cross buns. They were greatly inferior to the cakes my Mother provided every day, and probably only desirable because they came only once a year. Then there were chocolate Easter eggs which were inferior to common chocolate bars and much more expensive, but highly attractive to the eye. On Easter Sunday we always had a lunch of one of our own fat lambs. It was good, but I was not very partial to meat in those days, and did not realise that we always had 'Best English' every day.

All the earlier Easter recollections seem to concern food, and include a public tea held on Good Friday in the Sunday Schoolroom of the Wesleyan Chapel. There was a service in the chapel after tea things had been washed up, but Non-Conformists did not observe Good Friday with any great solemnity. There was no three-hour service of meditation earlier in the day, for the hours our Lord was on the cross, and no attempt to make it anything but a holiday. Children could play games and read books which were utterly banned on the Sabbath.

I must have been at least sixteen, with the First World

War at its worst, before Good Friday became holy, and Easter Sunday a 'sure and certain hope'. At first Wallace's Ground played no very great part except that life was returning to the land, whatever the date of Easter. Every day was a Good Friday in those years of blood and sacrifice and death. Equally the Resurrection and the Life seemed nearer and more believable in this Field than anywhere else.

In young manhood and middle-age there came muddled thoughts that the crown of thorns had blossomed, when the first flowers budded on the blackthorn. There was also a very mundane satisfaction in the quiet and solitude of the Ground, with no work going on, and no bustle of holiday crowds. It was perhaps a selfish feeling of superiority to know I could be alone in an overcrowded world, almost an escape from reality. The great advantage of being a countryman is knowing where to 'stand and stare' and it helps if he has some sort of right to be there. It would be marvellous to own Wallace's Ground, but it is a good second-best that my family have farmed it for over a century.

Writing about spring in the field cannot be done from memory. I started by suggesting that too much beauty could be overwhelming. Mercifully it is impossible to remember all the sensations of the speedy unfolding of hope. The warm sun, the gentle breeze, the colour, the fragrance, the cloud shadow, the blue distance, the bird song and the shape of the hills are too good. Words sound sentimental, drowsy and cloying, when the essence of the youth of the world is energy. From the first celandine to the coming of the swallows there are months when any day can be perfect, and spring might be claimed to go on till the coming of the swifts rather than of the swallows. This gives Wallace's Ground a spring stretching from late January to May 5th, which does not fit any calendar.

Everyone knows the infinite variations in the English climate, but it possibly takes a countryman to appreciate that in the job of farming very big allowances must be made concerning the uncertain date of spring. I have known one year in a lifetime when cows were grazing grass in Wallace's Ground in February, and three when there was no growth until late April. In 1970 snow fell on April 1st, which was after Easter in that year, and there was still death in the bitter east wind. Hay and other stored food had to be fed to sheep and cattle at the same rate as they had been provided all the winter. Such seasons ram home the fact that a reserve must always be carried from one year to another, especially since there is no guarantee of escaping a run of several late springs in a row.

Many farmers are convinced that the weather goes in cycles and that we are in the middle of a series of late spring. Apparently there is some scientific evidence for this, but personally I am very doubtful about it, and it is very difficult for the layman to collect figures. It is easy to get rainfall records, but these vary enormously from district to district. For instance '1968 was the wettest year since 1931 for England and Wales' . . . 'Scotland and Ireland had a generally dry year.' This is a quotation from *The Times*, and proves how restricted local conditions can be. Poets talk of 'soft, warm April rain', and April laughing one minute and weeping the next; with an anti-feminist description of such behaviour as similar to that of a young maiden.

I have known April in Wallace's Ground all my life, but have never spotted any cycle or trend. Some years the flowers and herbage have been early, but it seems to have little to do with rain, whether soft, warm or mixed with snow. Always the soil is sufficiently wet after snow. Always the soil is sufficiently wet after the winter to provide enough water for plants to grow. Other factors are much more important, with soil temperature most essential of all. Air temperature and sunshine have a big influence on warming up the soil. In addition there is the effect of light, the rapidly lengthening days, which is a subject about which we know very little. Possibly even less is known about light intensity, as opposed to hours of daylight.

Since my Father's day it has been possible to influence rates of growth, by sowing early breeds of herbage, and by supplementing with chemicals the plant food which soil bacteria are making from the rotting of the residues of dung, and of last year's crops. In essence all that this means is that when the soil is warm enough for growth we can hasten the speed, and the bulk of green stuff produced. Instead of a mere nibble of fresh grass it is possible to get enough to feed the cows without using any purchased food or stored grass. Winter rations may be cut from two to four weeks earlier than used to be the case. Yet all that this means is that we shall be earlier than Father used to be, given the same weather. He never knew if he would have good grazing on April 1st or not till April 30th. We do not know if we shall have it on March 7th or April 15th. There remains the farming essential of a surplus of forage being retained from previous years.

If I seem to over-stress this point it is because I have so often stood in Wallace's Ground and noticed how different is the behaviour of plants and animals. This is true not only of domesticated but of wild animals. Man plans when his sheep shall lamb and they do it on the appointed day whatever the weather. Breeding in the wild also seems much more tied to certain dates than is the germination of seeds or the start of vegetable growth. Probably in nature the lengthening of daylight hours is more important than warmth, or the availability of food in fixing breeding dates. An old legend has it that birds choose their mates on St Valentine's Day, February 14th. The bit of folk lore does not claim that they mate on this day, and it is only very roughly true of pairing. The only point of interest is that our forefathers noticed preparation for spring in the wild, not connected with warmth or rain, but with lengthening days.

Where warmth and rain are very much more important than light in the wild is during the first few weeks of life. There is an enormous loss in April and May if the weather is very bad. This is especially true of birds. Sometimes it may not be very important in cases when the species normally have more than one brood per year. An outside example is with wood pigeons who breed throughout the spring and summer, but frequently only rear the late July and August hatchings. With partridges one short period of an hour or two of rain may wipe out the very young birds for the whole season. Still, partridges are seldom seen in

Wallace's Ground, but their dependence on the weather underlines the fact that domesticated animals are even more in peril for a short time after birth.

If lambs are born in April in the Field it is a departure from the farming plan. Dorset Horn sheep usually lamb in October and this has long been the breed of the farm. On this hill an April lamb is an accident, a ram has got through a fence in December and joined some ewes or ewe lambs which were prepared to mate. With the Dorset Horn breed lambing twice per year is possible, and three times in two years is being done on a commercial scale. My nephew might try the intensified lambing system but so far he has stuck to the conventional once per annum.

For at least 60 years farmers have been trying to lamb the Dorset Horn more often than annually, and new knowledge on health and nutrition has probably made it feasible. The old snag was that a proportion of ewes were failing to conceive a second time, when the ram was put out. At least they did not all lamb, within, say, a month, so that the shepherd was faced with an endless worry of arranging food for lambs of all ages, and of ewes in every stage of pregnancy or lactation. This is more troublesome with sheep than with other forms of livestock. Cows are seen separately twice daily for milking and can be fed individually, pigs are normally confined in groups of one age. Adult sheep are normally in one flock, except just at lambing time, when there are groups at different stages. In one field may be those who will not lamb for several days. In a smaller enclosure those who look as if they will lamb that day or night. Next a very sheltered place, with some individual pens for the newly lambed, and finally the main grazing area where the ewes and lambs are safely launched on their new life.

Obviously the man in charge has less work and worry when all the ewes have lambed, and are reunited in one flock, or possibly in two if it is decided to feed ewes with twins more generously. When lambs are coming fast the shepherd may not leave them day or night, and snatches the odd hour of sleep with his clothes on. He expects this strain as part of his job, but is not overjoyed if it happens more often than once per annum, as it now does in the planned lambing system of three times in two years. He hates any breakdown in the eight month routine, which spread lambing still more, and such breakdowns used to be common.

My forecast is that increased sheep production is more likely to lead to encouraging multiple births, than to lambing oftener than once per annum. In any case many of our present breeds will only lamb in the spring, which is probably why the picture of a young lamb is a symbol of Easter for many people. Wallace's Ground does not know them, apart from the occasional accidents already mentioned. It is possible, however, to look over the rolling hills to flocks on neighbouring farms. Some of these are of other breeds than our white faced Dorset Horns, and many are hybrids. Speckled faces are common in the lambs, and some are jet black. In fact the old Hampshire Down breed was quite dark all over when born, although in a few weeks the body wool was white, with black hair only on the face and legs. Wales has an all black breed, which used to have a special value in providing wool for clerical habits.

Personally I share the liking of the photographers for a spring lamb with a white face, although this is sheer sentimentality. From the Field they can be seen on other farms miles away as white dots. 'Whiter than white' has a real meaning as applied to very young lambs, especially since their mother's wool is grey and a trifle tattered by April. At one time there was a fashion for artificially colouring the wool of ewes and rams going to shows or sales. Usually the sheep were dipped in colouring materials known as 'bloom dips', or a coloured powder was used. In Wallace's Ground I have seen our sale ewes in May powdered slightly brown, but this was not a wildly unnatural colour. The idea was to hide the natural staining from dirt and dried sweat. The custom with the Hampshire Down sheep on a neighbouring farm was to dip them in a bright yellow liquid, which was striking but wildly unnatural.

Wool buyers strongly objected to powders and bloom dips. The tinting did not really warp the opinions of buyers or show judges, and the wool merchants eventually won their case. Colouring is either banned or completely out of fashion, which is highly reasonable and right. There is, however, something missing from the Fair Grounds with the passing of rams coloured like tangerines. The nearest approach in these days is a slight touch of yellow in the fleeces of sheep from a belt of sandy soil west of the Field. I have no idea if this colour has become a natural dye in the wool, or if it is fine dust mixed with the fleece, and washable. Sheep from soils of the Midford Sands always take my eye, which may prove that our forefathers were not entirely foolish in using bloom colouring.

To the countryman May is the last month of spring although calendars stretch the Quarter from March 25th to June 24th. By the end of May the splendour of the flood of new life has settled into vigorous maturity. Dark, healthy green is the dominant colour in Wallace's Ground in hedges, pasture or crops. Only in recent years has the Field seen any form of crop harvest in May. Cultivated grass has been cut in May and preserved as silage for winter feeding. This cutting changes the dark green of herbage to a very light shade for a few days. The same change occurs when cattle are intensively grazed on a small daily plot enclosed by an electric fence. Green as a crop colour changes, or is changed in May much more than the dark tint of the hedges. When the Field is in barley, for instance, the beginning of May sees the soil almost bare, except for the most delicate green rows, where the cereal is just showing its first shoots. Very soon these cover the soil and the earth colour vanishes. Yet it may be that the level, green sea of crop is disturbed before high summer, when it will whiten to harvest. A casual look over the field in early May will only register the ordered rows of barley shoots. A farmer looks *into* the crop, just as he looks *into* a flock of sheep, and not merely over their serried backs. He is seeking for faults in both cases – for illness in sheep, and for disease or weeds in the crop.

Many weeds germinate at about the same time as the barley, and first appear as fragile shoots which give no hint of a malignant future. Later in the month there is no doubt about their presence, and of the speed with which they are depriving the crop of food and light. May sees a great deal of spraying against weeds, and this will alter the colour of the Field. The weeds will turn brown or grey, and there can be a slight check to the barley, with a little bleaching of some leaves.

Other crops sown in the field will grow fast in this month, and all may be altered in colour by cultivations or by sprays against diseases or weeds. Potatoes, for instance, will be earthed up, which gardeners usually call 'round hoeing'. The soil in the centre of each drill is thrown up round the plants, with the object of killing weeds between the drills, and of providing loose, fine earth near the stem, where the tubers will grow. This changes the colour of the Field, and gives a short return, between dark green rows, of that rich shade of newly moved earth.

Examples of spraying against diseases and weeds can be seen in kale, grown for cow food in early autumn. The first seedlings may be attacked in May by flea beetles which bore shot holes in the leaves. This spray does not influence the colour of crop or soil immediately, but saves the kale from a bad check, or extinction. A more spectacular treatment on kale is when a weed called fat hen is found growing with it. Kale is a fast grower, and can get on top of most weeds, but fat hen can smother it. The very broad leaf of kale makes it susceptible to many weed killers, but a few selective chemicals have been discovered. Even with these the kale may be distinctly checked. The usual procedure is to let the fat hen grow with the kale until the weed is above the crop, and about one foot high. Then by spraying on a dry day the weedicide stays mainly on the leaves of the fat hen. At least twenty-four hours without rain is necessary for full success, which involves the dying back of the fat hen, and only a slight scorching of the kale. The look of the crop just after treatment is sufficient to cause the least interested visitor to stand and stare. There is no shadow of doubt that modern science has been indulging in some dubious chemical trick.

Such weed killing is not cheap, but the farmer knows that the alternative of hand hoeing is impossibly more expensive. In some ways it can be compared with using costly machines to do jobs which 20 years ago were done by human toil. To me one difference is that the new machines often do a better job whereas weed killers sometimes are only fairly successful.

In Wallace's Ground on a long May evening I do not like the faintest suggestion of a trace of chemical in the air. I am not afraid it will do me the slightest harm, and I do not mind the stronger smell of a newly carted dung heap by the gate. It is merely alien to the Field. I dislike equally the smell of freshly spread liquid manure, and of the small trickle of effluent coming from a silage clamp. Both the latter are natural smells, as natural as the blue wood smoke from the valley, where the elderly save electricity by lighting a few logs in the cool of the day.

There are times when I am not completely logical in wanting Wallace's Ground unchanged, and the worst time of weakness is in the evening of a perfect spring day.

Chapter Four

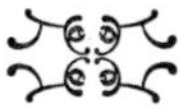

Life Established

I found it difficult to define dates for the beginning and ending of spring in Wallace's Ground, for the first stirring of life is very early, and the last blossoming can overlap the first harvest of grass as silage. Summer presents the same difficulty, and the only certainty is that what the calendar calls Midsummer, June 24th, is not the middle of a period of established life.

Summer is a season when development takes place, after the madly wasteful competition of spring. This is reasonably true of the wild life of plants and animals in the hedges and banks. The birds which have survived hatching and fledging are likely to grow in fair safety. The young hare can fight off or out-distance most predators. The flowers are through the competition for light, and will mature to form seeds, although heaven knows how many seeds will ever grow. In the tamed Field man has established his dominance. Plants 'grow as they are told', and domestic animals lead the life man has planned for them.

This at least is the first superficial impression of Wallace's Ground in Summer. Food production is taking place under controlled conditions. Factories and farms always had a good deal in common, and it is strange that 'factory farming' should have become a term of reproach, merely because of changes in method. The old wheelwright's factory has developed into the motorcar works. The increase of one wheat grain by forty-fold is rather less spectacular, since Grandfather sometimes got ten fold. Yet neither the work of the wheelwright, nor of the farmer was ever remotely natural. The hen in a cage may now lay nearly 300 eggs per year. Mother's free ranging flock only managed a third of this number, but 100 eggs per year is clean outside nature. My nephew averages 1,000 gallons of milk per cow per annum, whereas my Father was lucky to get 500, yet no wild bison ever got near this lower figure. All farming is unnatural, and in summer in Wallace's Ground I become very conscious of it.

This is the season when the vast increase in crops is visibly taking place under the open sky. In glasshouses men control the climate and the growth of plants. Just as by housing animals they alter environment and food. Both controlled temperature and light are costly, and cater for a new expansion of prosperity in Britain. Here in the summer of the Field the mounting production goes back to the days when some Celtic slave grew bread. The modern use of chemical weedkillers and fertilisers is only a small step beyond the primitive attempt to grow millions of one sort of seeding grass, wild wheat, and nothing else. Not a little of the success or failure of the crop is still due to factors outside man's control.

Long spells of rain or of drought will lead to smaller crops. The weather will have a great influence on plant disease, and on insect attack. Summer in Wallace's Ground can be as cheering or as depressing today as it was when the Romans took a tribute of wheat grain. Progress in production is real enough, but there is a limit when human skill is beaten by nature. My Father would have been amazed at the speed with which crops can be harvested by modern machines. It is a triumph that the whole Field can be harvested, threshed and the grain stored in the barn given one fine day. Yet the great combine harvester can still stand impotent, covered with tarpaulins, without that one fine day. It could be the same story as in 1860, in Grandfather's time, when the grain was never cut. Incidentally, my Grandfather also told me that 1860 was the season when the reaper was invented, although he did not see one for several years thereafter.

To me it has always seemed ironic that a big step forward was made in the speed of harvest in the very year when harvest on our Dorset hills was impossible. Man invents, probes, and reduces risks, but in the end 'God giveth the increase'.

For modern readers it may be necessary to define the name 'reaper'. Grandfather was quite right about the date, but the word has been used somewhat loosely. It has been applied to the first reciprocating blade mowing machine for grass, which was invented by a Scottish clergyman in 1826, but was not in common use in 1850, when Grandfather was farming. In addition 'reaper' is often used today for 'self-binder', which only became common in the present century. I saw my first in a field adjoining Wallace's Ground about 1907, and it seemed a marvellous invention. It cut the grain, bundled it into a sheaf, tied it with twine, cut the string, and threw it safely clear to allow the next circuit of the field. Not being mechanical, I have never followed quite just how that knot is tied, but the rest of the machine is nakedly understandable. The present self-binders are used when unbruised wheat straw is needed for thatch. Combine harvesters chew up the straw to some extent.

The modern binder is still a thoroughly Heath Robinson contraption, with moving canvas, clattering chains, and short forks which suddenly throw out the sheaf at exactly the right moment. The machine looks as if some of the activity, powered by one large wheel in contact with the earth, will inevitably drop into chaos at any moment. Instead they seem to be virtually indestructible. Grandfather's reaping machine cut the crop and threw it clear of the next circuit of the machine, but did not tie a knot. The sheaves were made by hand, using a handful of straw instead of twine. Such tying was done by a peculiar twist of the wrist, which left the ears of the bond hanging down, where they would quickly dry after rain. It was a tiny bit of skill which had lasted ever since men first tied a sheaf. Last year in Wallace's Ground I was one of three men who tried to tie a straw bond, and found we had lost the knack, which once seemed to be born in us.

On a summer day the activity of men in the Field varies enormously with the crop being grown. With wheat and barley everything has been done which can influence the crop. Weeds have already been killed by chemicals, or the weather has interfered at the time of spraying, and some pests have escaped. Almost inevitably the spread of weed killer has not been wholly uniform. Human attention wanders, a spray nozzle chokes, and is unnoticed, or the driver of the sprayer strays. The missed patch has a fascination for the farmer. If it shows a smother of weeds he congratulates himself on his wisdom in spraying. If the weeds are few his mind goes to the cost of chemical of about 30s. per acre, plus haulage and labour. Also where the sprayer has overlapped, and given a double dose, he may even have spent good money and damaged his crop.

I have seen Wallace's Ground in summer when spraying misses have left bright yellow strips of charlock, and the clean state of the rest of the crop has seemed to prove that spraying has paid. This happens so often with charlock and poppies that many farmers spray as a regular routine as an insurance, and I think I agree with them. There is, however, a new spirit in farming, which goes far beyond the factory search for new processes and chemicals.

I have sneered in my time at people who have called farming 'a way of life'. I have protested that I am a scientist and a businessman. 'A way of life' claimant has sometimes proved to be a bit of a crank. He longs for a return to Nature – always with a capital N – and has a number of mixed vices and virtues, all of a minority type. There seems no reason why being vegetarian, disliking chemical fertilisers, blood sports, pesticides, shaving, and conventional clothing should occur in one person, but they often do.

My claim that farming is fundamentally different from town industry gives a different meaning to 'a way of life'. Farming is far out in front in one pattern of modern thought. Having once followed strictly orthodox methods, inherited for generations, agriculture now doubts everything. The new is questioned, and the industries connected with farming have to search rather desperately for answers.

For instance, I said the yellow unsprayed strips in Wallace's Ground proved that the weed killer had been successful. This seems obvious until some young farmer comes along and says 'how much actual loss is caused by having charlock in barley'. The scientists then do accurate experiments, and find that it takes a very heavy infestation to cause a serious reduction in yield, or at least that there is no very spectacular increase in returns to pay for the extra cost.

This does not please the industrial maker of chemicals, although he eventually comes up with a perfectly true list of secondary reasons for weed killing. The major point in advertising literature is still 'highest possible returns', but this is immediately followed by 'indirect advantages'. These stress easier harvesting, cleaner grain and less artificial drying of combined corn. In addition it is claimed that killing weeds before they seed reduces the danger to future crops.

The questing minds of farmers accept none of the old art of husbandry as sacred, nor the much publicised new miracles of science. In some ways the research workers and teachers of today are in much the same position as the Ministers of religion. There are few traditionally faithful, but happily even less complete unbelievers, by which I mean real 'factory farmers'. Farming is a way of life because it is still a very individual occupation, and a strange new youth searches for truth in this oldest of activities.

Leaning on the gate of Wallace's Ground I look at my Nephew's crops, which are far better and cleaner than my Brother, my Father, or Grandfather ever grew. Obviously new methods are being used, and yet I know that he is not satisfied with the 'fairy tales of science, or the long results of time'. He has doubts of the old plough, and of the weed killers, the placing of fertiliser in the rows with the seed, and strengthening of straw by a spray which checks its growth, and whether mildew in the barley leaves should be controlled by a chemical which enters the sap.

In my youth I have said that Wallace's was in permanent grass, but the soil in adjoining fields is very similar, and I have cultivated, sown and harvested in all of them. Looking at the barley it seems very near perfection to me, especially on a hot, still day when a tiny breeze sets the ears rippling, right across to the further hedge, and there is a sound of a gentle rustle which promises abundance. I am content.

Time was when I accepted farm work as inevitable toil, based on unchanging rules of good husbandry. Then came questioning, searching for new ideas, experimenting and never feeling I had found the whole answer. Now, for me, it is less necessary to search for complete understanding of every detail. There is a valid comparison in speaking of my farming teachers, and of ministers and priests. Once I accepted all I was told in Sunday School, and in the regular twice daily service on Sundays. Then came doubts, and a period of trying almost every way of life and new doctrine. Finally, the feeling I mentioned earlier that 'God giveth the increase' however clever or stupid I may have become. A summer day, with Wallace's Ground in barley, is made perfect because I can accept and be thankful. It may sound as if I have become too old for striving, and am merely willing to accept anything which requires no rational thought. Rather naturally I prefer the other explanation that a man can go through stages of humanism, of self-indulgence and of getting near atheism, and come out on the other side.

Leaning on the gate in high summer produces completely different feelings when Wallace's Ground is in different crops than cereals. The content remains, but not the mood of quietly waiting for harvest. The tractors may be busy cultivating, or sowing kale as late as mid-July. Only when they stop at lunchtime does any drowsy peace return. The swifts scream through the sky. They fly high in settled weather, but skim the hedges when showers are coming. It is just possible that a skylark may be singing, but most of the birds are silent. At least they are no longer making the pleasant noises we regard as song. To a countryman there is something amusing about the scientific description of bird song. This is 'Any audible performance linked with breeding, courtship or territory holding.'

There is no doubt that this is true also of the noises made

by rooks, corncrakes and night-jars, which is hardly song in the human sense. At least it is not what my generation think of as 'song', but then to us some human music is no more than a noise. Perhaps the scientists are right in defining bird song; it is only old-fashioned poets who think the larks, blackbirds, thrushes and nightingales are enjoying themselves. Poets use phrases such as 'Birds at the break of day chant their morning prayers,' or 'The first fine careless rapture,' or 'Panted forth a flood of rapture so divine,' and of the nightingale's song 'Charmed magic casements, opening on the foam of perilous seas, in faery lands forlorn.'

I think I prefer the poets to the naturalists, although, to be fair, one scientist did tell me that he thought blackbirds got pleasure from singing.

When the tractors pause at lunchtime in the cultivation of kale there may be no bird song, but not necessarily a bird silence. Blackbirds are outstanding in doing a great deal of talking which is not concerned with mating. They can explode from a nearby bush if they suddenly decide you are a shade too close, and depart with a shriek of fear. The more unobtrusively a poacher moves in daylight the more certain he is to have his presence revealed by blackbirds.

They have another curious voice which is used mainly when fledglings have just left the nest. The adult bird will keep up an endless series of chirps on one note. There is something irritating about this insistant noise, which certainly seems to influence cats. Possibly it has the same effect on the cat as it does on me. I find myself watching the adult bird and following it to see what the fuss is about. The result is that the chirping leads me into the next field, well away from the almost helpless fledgling. The blackbird stops the noise, ceases the slow movement from branch to branch, and flies away silently as soon as I am remote from her young. I have seen my own cat tricked in exactly the same way. It is on a par with the partridge, who will give a convincing act of having a broken wing to lead a predator away from her offspring. On the other hand, a peewit will swoop, screaming, to within inches of your head, to keep your eyes off the ground.

Apart from these bird noises associated with fear, the typical sound at midday in midsummer is the hum of insects, varied by a high pitched ping as a mosquito swoops. Flies can be an infernal nuisance on a close thundery day, and provide an excuse for tobacco. Actually, having been a heavy smoker I now know that smoke is not much of a deterrent. A scarf sprayed from the kitchen aerosol is much more effective, although someone is almost sure to discover that any really effective spray is poisoning me. If so I shall buy a large stock of spray before it is banned, and maintain some protection against annoyance.

The nuisance of flies in Wallace's Ground is much less than in small valley fields. It is at its worst at lunchtime with the tractor stopped, but never half as bad as it was in the old horse days. Horse sweat seemed to be even more attractive than human. We left their tails long, of course, and covered their ears with little hoods. When turned loose on Sundays they stood in pairs, head to tail, and kept the flies off each other. Tied up at lunchtime on working days they could not practice this very sensible co-operation.

In addition to the annoyance of crawling flies there was also the chance of a painful bite from very large flies. These were called horse or gad flies, presumably because horses were liable to gad or bolt when stung. The sting on humans was not only painful but apt to fester. Actually it is inaccurate to describe their attack as either biting or stinging, although it is a human reaction. What happens is that the female gad fly pierces the skin and sucks blood.

They always were much more common in small valley fields, and I have not been worried by them in Wallace's Ground for quite a few years. Rather unexpectedly this was nothing to do with the disappearance of the horse. If only we had known about the life history of the fly in my youth we could have controlled the nuisance on the hills with fair ease. At the time the best the scientists could offer was to rub the horse with paraffin and soap. This deterrent did not deter, nor did it work on humans or cattle.

Probably the worst place for gad flies today is on swampy land such as the Dorset Heath, or the New Forest. When we had it in Wallace's Ground the whole trouble was the muddy pond in the far corner. With the pond dry, and only deep water in troughs, the nuisance has vanished, unless an odd female fly follows you up the hill from the valley. I find it pleasant to know that the male gad fly leads a blameless life, feeding on pollen and nectar. The female is the blood sucker, and she lays her eggs on damp ground on the borders of swamps or streams. Hence the connection of our pond with this pest.

Even if we had possessed knowledge of the life history of the fly we might still have retained the pond, and done nothing about it. To destroy the insects at the point of hatching from the pond would have meant treating the water with paraffin early in summer. Since we had no supply of piped water in those days it would have meant making the only source of drinking water unpalatable at the time when we needed it most. By this I mean that in winter the horses could drink from the stream in the valley before and after work. They ploughed from 7 a.m. to 2.30 p.m. with a short break for oats and chaff from their nosebags. There was no need for a drink during this spell, in cool conditions. It was quite a different story at haymaking time when normal hours were from 7 a.m. to 8 p.m. and liable to stretch a bit later. There was an absolute need for the horses to drink about 1 p.m. Without the pond they would have had the unnecessary labour of walking right down the hill and back. This would have cut half-an-hour off their lunch rest – and mine if I was acting carter boy.

Gad flies suck the blood of cattle as well as of humans and of horses. I have not seen the pest in Wallace's Ground now for a long time, but this does not prevent the heifers from having sudden fits of wild galloping. It seems certain that they will run for any insect that approaches them making a vicious humming noise. This must be inherited fear to some extent, and panic is infectious. Plenty of the heifers grazing Wallace's Ground when it is in ley have never been stung by a gad fly. They can have no personal memories connecting buzzing with pain. Instinct plays strange tricks. I have never been bitten by a snake, but their hiss has produced fear on the few occasions I have disturbed them. It could be that the hiss of a gander is more frightening than its threatening wings.

Cultivating the Field at mid-summer always arouses my wonder at the enormous effect it must be having on the world of millions of tiny creatures in the soil. Inverting and stirring the top few inches of earth changes their world at any season, but never more than when life is established, and growth at its speediest. Here is a jungle, with close cropped grass appearing to tower like mighty trees. A spider throws a suspension bridge between two blades of grass. Underground centipedes move in the darkness and fasten to the bodies of their prey. The jungle is alive with innumerable bodies far smaller than spiders or centipedes. Millions of bodies reproducing, starving, dying, reproducing, destroying each other and always reproducing. They are the living things, the little uncomplicated shapes which are bacteria of disease, of change, of redistribution.

With the plough the forest is overthrown. Light is admitted to one population, and darkness comes suddenly to another. Air is admitted freely, stimulating some life and destroying other. Even smaller than bacteria is the virus, which is also revolutionised by the change of light, air and moisture. We can describe the shape of bacteria, seen under the microscope, in terms of spheres, rods and cones. Of the virus it is hard to say anything except that it is something alive, something which can twist the growth of plants or kill an animal with disease. Once we had foot-and-mouth disease in Wallace's Ground, and that is due to a virus. It is the most highly infectious animal disease known. In humans influenza is a virus disease, and I remember climbing the hill to the Field and collapsing at the top, after having apparently recovered from the vile illness. This smallest form of life is least under the domination of man. Apart from foot-and-mouth disease, the viruses are responsible for rabies, swine fever, distemper in dogs, and fowl pest.

A microbe, a fungus, and every other form of life seems capable of a separate existence, as spores or egg. The viruses must always have living tissue to live on and one way of preserving them for study is in a fertilised hen egg placed in an incubator.

The plough tears through a world. It is doing what we know an H bomb could do to our cities. A little science can put morbid thoughts into the mind of a man, which are alien to Wallace's Ground on a summer day.

When Wallace's Ground is in grass for a few years there are other variants of the reaction it has on me. These are complicated by the fact that the grass may be cut as a crop to be conserved for the winter, or it may be grazed with sheep or cattle.

Grazing may start very early in spring, or it may be after May 1st, before there is any growth. May, 1970, was an example of the latter. In that year the flowering of the hedges was late, but not quite as late as the springing of the grass. As a result the cows had their first bite of natural food at the peak of wild beauty. The blackthorn was a miracle, and the first green of the grass was something which is never quite repeated later in the summer.

The sheep had been out all the winter and were feeling a certain amount of discomfort from the spring itch of their coats. Even in the mild Dorset climate May is a bit early for shearing. In any case the ewes in Wallace's Ground were being given the best quality grass available. The Field is not rich by valley standards, but is one of the best bits of soil on a naturally poor farm. These favoured ewes were the older members of the flock, who were due to be sold at the great breed sale on the second Thursday of May. The good eating probably made their fleeces more itchy, and put them in some danger in the early summer sunshine. The natural reaction of most animals with an itchy back is to roll, and sheep are unfortunate in that if they reach the point of being flat on their backs they are completely unable to turn over. If they remain in this position with all four feet in the air, they will die. If their heads are downhill, death may come in well under the hour, so fat sheep, near shearing time, need a lot of watching, but it is a tradition to send them to Dorchester May Sale 'in their wool'.

The likeliest time for itching and rolling is about midday

or at least in the hours when the sun is really hot. If you are caught by a farmer trespassing in a field with sheep, it is a perfect answer to say you thought you saw one on its back. They need not be fat sheep, and the weather need not be hot, because they could easily get stuck in a small depression in the turf. Incidentally, if you ever do see four legs in the air, first tie your dog to the gate, then turn the sheep over, but hang on to it for a few minutes if you possibly can. It will certainly be scared and giddy, which will make it stagger away at a run. This may mean that it will blunder into something and hurt itself. I have known a ewe, which was fairly far gone, stagger away at a gallop, and then drop dead. Presumably the reason was a very sudden strain on the heart, but I do not know. For that matter I have looked through half a dozen books on sheep, and on diseases of sheep, without finding why they die on their backs. Every sheep farmer must have lost some in his time, but the nearest I can get to an answer is that I once stuck and skinned one which was very near death. All I found, on opening it up, was considerable congestion of the lungs. How many men sleep on their backs, and snore, with no influence on *their* comfort?

Shepherd always used to erect an arrangement in Wallace's Ground which was alleged to enable the sheep to rub their backs without rolling. On many farms it is thought to be enough to drive a few very stout posts vertically into the soil. These allow the sheep to rub, but shepherds thought they might not be able to get at the very centre of their backs with a mere scratching post. His contraption consisted of two stout posts connected with a horizontal bar. The sheep could crouch a little under this bar, or arch their backs up if they were very short in the leg. It certainly gave them the chance of getting a real rub, and they certainly enjoyed it. I have never been sure that it stopped the tendency to roll, or reduced the danger of losses 'on-the-back'. We all know a cat is liable to have a sudden, imperative need to scratch itself at any moment. The same urge could come to a sheep when it was some distance from the official rubbing bar.

When the Field is grazed with cattle in summer they are possibly less comfortable than they used to be. The machine clipped hedges of today are low and offer little shade. Modern grazing management lays it down that the cows should be fairly closely confined. By moving an electric fence every day the cows get a fresh bite of grass, which is efficient rationing. It does stop them wandering, however, and their chance of finding shade is greatly reduced.

In my youth, when the sun beat down, the cattle stopped grazing completely for hours on end. Nothing would tempt them out of the shade, except the need for a drink, and cows can do without a drink for a very long time. They can swallow well over a dozen gallons of water without raising their heads, which goes far beyond the best efforts of human beer drinkers. The restlessness of cows, in small paddocks without shade, is a comparatively new thing in Wallace's Ground.

It is rather appropriate in this case to quote the Old Testament – 'There is no new thing under the sun.' The island of Jersey has had the problem of cows being worried in the sun for many generations. Their tethering of cattle separately on a fresh patch every day was probably not fundamentally to get more efficient grazing, although it was sound management. I think it arose because land in Jersey was too valuable to waste on stock-proof hedges. It was impossible to turn the animals loose in a field, or even to drive them along a road back home for milking. They had to be led along the road and tethered in the field. In the Field at home the control of grazing by small paddocks is purely to graze and fertilise in succession, to get more grass. Yet the final result is the same as in Jersey; the cows are out in the midday sun.

At present we are not showing much sign of accepting the Jersey answer to the problem. At least one reason why Jersey cows go out to graze in summer wearing overcoats is to reduce annoyance from flies. Another is that Jersey farmers used to rely to a fairly large extent on selling cows as well as bulls for export. The world went back to the Island far more than it does now for the basic blood of the breed. In modern days there has been an import of Danish Jerseys to England. When Island export was very widespread it was important that a cow or bull should look at its best all the time. The Jersey farmer never had any long warning of when a foreign buyer might arrive. The cloths were worn to keep the coat of the animal in Show condition.

It was unfortunate that the covering of the grazing cattle in Jersey led many farmers to the completely false conclusion that the animals were delicate. The question of warmth had nothing to do with the wearing of overcoats, but it certainly gave considerable protection from the nuisance of flies. Since we seem unlikely to use overcoats it seems that the hope in Wallace's Ground is the discovery of a cheap and efficient fly repellent. There are very sound reasons why it would pay to be able to get cows to graze quietly in the heat of the day. Any stress of irritation is bad for the farmer since the milk yield falls.

There might seem to be a case for letting the hedges grow tall again, especially the long one which borders the Field on the south. Actually we had a drop in yields in the old days when there was a long period of sunny weather. The cows were lying quietly in the shade, without the restlessness they now show, when forced to stay in the glare. The trouble is that they were not eating grass. Apparently they do not make up for missing a meal by gorging more in the cool of the day.

It is faulty memory to think of leaning on the gate on a summer day and feeling a little perturbed by the obvious irritation of the cows in their small, temporary paddocks. This certainly has happened to me but not on many days. In early summer the flies are seldom bad, and the cows graze happily through most of May. Fly trouble is intensified in June, but on many days there is cloud and, occasionally, continuous rain. It is very easy to exaggerate both the hot sun and the continuous rain. What is much more common at midday in mid-summer, in Wallace's Ground, is fairly cool shade. This has no great influence on the time spent in grazing.

Last summer I remember leaning on the middle gate of

the Field and thinking idly about grazing. Earlier I wrote that my nephew's crops of corn are so much better than any my Father ever grew that the sight of them is very pleasant. Considering how important grass is in this country it is a bit surprising that grazing still presents a number of problems. There have been vastly improved varieties of grasses, considerable increases in yield through fertilisers, and better returns from giving a fresh patch for feeding every day. There has been advance, but every chart showing the value of grazing still shows an enormous drop in summer. This is not when the cold stops growth, or when a drought checks it. Irrigation will not prevent it, and it happens when soil temperature, light intensity, and day length still seem favourable for growth. In fact the summer plunge is followed by an autumn recovery in the value the cows get from grazing.

The feeding value of pasture falls when the grass would be producing a seed head. It is understandable that if a head is formed the grass should transfer food from the leaves to the seeds where it is not palatable to cows. What is still a little strange is that we can prevent head formation by topping with a mower, yet the feeding value will still fall about the middle of June until early August. On well managed grass a cow will produce five gallons of milk per day in May without extra food. Yet in a fortnight from mid-June onwards the grass is only good for three gallons or less. If we continue to feed a five gallon cow on grass alone she will lose body weight and then drop her yield.

The best that science had achieved is to shorten the period of low feeding value, but there remains a drop at midsummer, although the grass may still look leafy and green. The recovery in late August never reaches the feeding values of May. On average Wallace's Ground will produce five gallons of milk per cow for the two months from April 15th to June 15th. After June cake will have to be fed for each gallon over the third, and it will have to be cake rich in protein. In August it is wise still to give supplementary food for each gallon over three, but it need not be expensive protein cake. A relatively cheap starchy mixture of maize or barley can be substituted.

It is impossible to give any accurate date when grazing is likely to cease. The feeding value of the herbage will not fall very seriously after August, but the quantity of grass depends on drought and on early frost. Over the years the Field gives some cattle food from, say, April 15th to October 15th. This is fairly good for the nature of the soil and the altitude, yet it is not under control in the sense that corn yields have been standardised.

I like watching sheep or cattle grazing in Wallace's Ground when it is having its rotation in grass. There is much more herbage than when it was in permanent pasture in my youth, and it is better herbage. Yet the Field in grass manages to remind me that this is basically a thin, poor soil. Probably these chalk uplands have increased their sale price as land far more than much better soils. My native farm would probably sell for £250 per acre against not more than £15 in 1939. First class permanent pasture in the neighbouring Vale was worth £100 per acre in 1939 but not much more than £300 today. For the last fifteen years growing crops had been more profitable than milk production or fattening cattle, and Wallace's Ground is very easy to cultivate hence the enormous rise in value.

My nephew can fertilise to grow cereals which could not be bettered, on any soil, which brings me back to the obstinate fact that pasture is not under control to the same extent. The Field will never have the density of herbage, of the fattening pasture of nearby Hammoon. When a cow sweeps her tongue round a bite she will not get as many grass leaves and, remember, cows graze for a fairly rigid length of time per day. The soil will dry out quicker than in the Vale, and irrigation is not feasible on the hills under present laws about water supplies. I am very content with the Field in grain, but vaguely dissatisfied with modern science when it is in grass.

This applies less to cutting grass for silage or hay, than to grazing. The herbage before cutting can look as lush as anything in the Vale, although the actual yield will probably be less. I have learned from experience that I usually underestimate the yield from, say, the red soils of East Devon, because of long familiarity with Wallace's Ground. It will grow very reasonable yields, but recovery after cutting is less reliable than on the deep soils. When the soil is exposed to the sun after cutting the surface tends to bake, although one week of cloudy, moist weather is enough to get it covered again.

On good soils the denser herbage protects new growth from burning, but this is only true on deep, friable soils. Clay may burn as badly as thin chalk, and it may also crack in deep fissures as it shrinks in the sun. The desiccation in the Field and the cracking on clay are both made worse by modern machinery. The new mowers and silage cutters get a lot nearer the earth than we ever could in the past. The result is a very short grass stubble with precious little shading of the exposed soil.

Another point is that the old permanent pasture contained a great number of different grasses and clovers, some of which have far deeper roots than the very few species we sow on temporary grass fields. On average it is not worth buying the seed of grasses whose main virtue is that they can withstand drought. An example is the grass cocksfoot, which is not very palatable and not very digestible, but will be the only green thing if we get a fortnight's scorching days after cutting for hay and silage.

I have occasionally watched Wallace's Ground rather sadly in July, when it has looked quite barren, but probably not more often than one year in ten. The answer to the problem is one of the oldest things in agriculture. If a man knows his soil he can manage it to fit its limitations. The last outermost realms of intensification can be left to the pioneering odd genius. This is a dangerous sphere where the weather may beat the best modern methods. The ordinary successful farmer uses fertilisers, and new grassland management, but always with a margin of safety.

Wallace's Ground will grow one good crop of grass sometime between the middle of May and the first half of June. That is a safe basis for the number of sheep and cattle the farm will carry through next winter. Quite possibly two or three cuts of silage could be taken before the middle of

August, but on this soil grass can only be trusted for one large crop. Intensification is known to be possible with green material other than grass. I have seen sainfoin in the Field, and I am fairly sure it would grow lucerne. Both these plants of the clover family have deep roots, and are impervious to drought, although not very happy in very wet conditions.

An attempt to push up cow numbers might be connected with making silage three times per annum from sainfoin in Wallace's Ground, or by cutting a barley crop for silage just before it was ripe. It could be done, but it would complicate life.

This statement is enough to stir all citizens who think farmers are 'feather-bedded' and I apologise. It certainly sounds as if a quiet, unthinking life is the aim. This is certainly not true and especially not about young and middle-aged men today. My meaning is that complicating life to keep a few more cows could be unprofitable on the farm taken as a whole. The old simplicity is gone for ever, and extra operations usually involve more labour or more machinery. How many extra cows would justify one extra man, and how near is the milking lay-out to saturation point?

At the moment Wallace's Ground fits into a farm with three major enterprises – corn, milk and out-of-season lamb. Sometimes it is cultivated, and sometimes sown to herbage mixtures. Specialising only in either cows or sheep would be expensive, and dangerous, or would render much equipment unwanted. To make the whole farm a dairy enterprise would involve another set of buildings, a motor-road, and the purchase of another hundred cows at about £100 each. This is expensive. A switch to intensive grain would be dangerous from the point of view of plant disease. Concentration on sheep would render cultivating and harvesting implements unwanted, and the present milking accommodation would not convert easily to grain stores, or sheep housing.

Actually no man would be the least bit likely to try only intensive sheep on this easy working land. Sheep can be a break from recurring grain crops, or the only way of farming sheep mountains. A farm consisting of fields like Wallace's

Ground could never be used wholly for sheep under any system known to me, under any predictable price structure. What would seem a more likely happening is that the sheep should be dropped, leaving only two major enterprises – milk and corn. It is true that milk might become less profitable in the near future, if there is a big change in public buying of the daily fresh bottles. Various preserved milks are much nearer to having the taste of fresh, and long keeping makes imports possible. Stressing the fact that dried skimmed milk is 'slimming' or 'fat free' is another danger, as long as the taste makes no great difference to tea or to coffee.

A sudden serious slump in milk, however, is not very likely, and cow keeping combined with corn growing would leave Wallace's Ground much as it is at present. Slipping quietly out of sheep might pay my nephew, and leave me with no great feeling of change and decay. Sometimes the Field would be in grass and sometimes in corn. I should miss the sheep on the farm as a whole, but they have never been grazed much on this land, except just before May Sale. The Ground has always been near enough to the village for the use of more profitable young cattle, and the sheep were in distant fields at greater altitudes.

There is a tendency to think of spring as the time for flowers, but late May must be counted as summer, and many plants do not blossom until after the middle of the month. May 25th was Bank Holiday in 1970 and I spent the afternoon in Wallace's Ground. The hawthorn was not in bloom, although the buds opened three days later. The hedges had thickened after the trimming of last autumn, and looked solid green barriers. Quite a bit of this was not real fencing shrubs, but a vulnerable growth of tall couch grass and sprawling herbs. In the lane climbing up to the Field one hedge was untrimmed. Here dandelions were in full flower in the gutter, followed by a fringe of sheep's parsley halfway up the bank. These were very beautiful, and regular enough to look as if they had been planted. There seems no reason why they should not last for posterity. The lane is wide enough for any farming purpose and the verge will be untouched unless some housing estate agent decides to 'develop' this steep hill.

The lacey sheeps' parsley has always been in the lane hedge and not inside Wallace's Ground. Presumably the reason is because sheep like it, and will graze it very hard in the Field during May if they have access to a hedge bank. Perhaps I was premature in saying that the Field would be unchanged for me if the farm had no flock. A delicate fringe of white blossom would not hurt the hedge as a fence, and I know where to expect it. Sheeps' parsley loves sunshine and the hedge it would colonise would be the one facing south.

Another more unexpected blossom in the lane hedge bank was a small clump of bluebells. For some reason I have never noticed these in the past. Perhaps I have always been too busy to stand and stare, and it was a very small clump. One villager taking the dog for a walk could pick the lot, and not have a very large bunch. It was nothing like the miles of blue fringing some Devon roads. Very possibly those few bluebells have appeared for many years without my mind recording them. It sounds impossible, but it is a fact that busy people tend to miss sights, sounds and smells when they are preoccupied with work.

On the whole farmers are not good naturalists. They tend to look only at the crops or the animals, registering what work is necessary and planning how it shall be done. If the bluebells had been there in my childhood I would have noticed them, just as I noticed birds' nests. Later, as a science student, I saw loose smut on wheat, a misshapen udder on a cow, or a restless sheep twitching its tail. The latter is a sign of that rather ghastly bit of nature, in which flies may settle on soiled wool, and their maggots eat the live flesh of sheep.

I still see ills in crops and animals which are overlooked by town visitors, but a divorce from farm work leaves time to see colour, to smell honeysuckle, and to hear sounds which have no connection with making a living. Fifty years ago I would have noticed if old Ike Collins had stopped ploughing in Wallace's Ground, because his unoiled plough wheels had ceased to squeak. But at that time I should not have noticed that the wheatears had joined the birds of the Field in March.

Farm workers are much more likely to notice wild life. At least they were in my youth when farm 'labourer' was a fair description. They were doing what they were told, not planning for tomorrow, and most jobs involved physical effort rather than concentration. It was a farm worker who first showed me a wheatear in March. I do not think they ever bred on our farm, but had paused after crossing the sea on their way to semi-waste land such as Mendip or the northern heather. The best time to see them in Wallace's Ground was in late September, when they flocked on our hills near the coast, rather in the way swallows congregate on telephone wires before starting south.

At one time a shepherd on the farm got quite a few shillings by snaring wheatears for food, usually in late September. They must have made a poor meal because they are smaller than the quail, our smallest game bird. A partridge is no more than a good meal for a healthy man, and the wheatear is less than a quarter the size of a partridge. I have never eaten a wheatear and cannot discuss their flavour. They and their eggs are now completely protected by an Act passed in 1954 and, fortunately, this is one law which is reasonably well enforced. It sounds incredible that a bird smaller than a blackbird should ever have been eaten, but in fact sparrow pie was once consumed by the very poor. Trapping sparrows, by methods now illegal, were well known to children in my boyhood. I think this had little to do with sparrow pie, but went back to a very old method of pest control.

Without any doubt house sparrows are a pest to farmers, and gardeners. At harvest time I have seen wheat stripped by them, and the straw broken by the weight of flocks of these small birds. In spring they damage garden crops, and seem to do wanton harm in destroying the petals of polyanthus flowers. At first sight it seems unusual to get corn damage in Wallace's Ground, which is remote from the village. House sparrows seldom go far from human dwellings. The answer lies in the block of old farm sheds in the field immediately next to the Ground. It is at this east end of the enclosure that crop damage can be bad.

Unfortunately no one has discovered any legal method of keeping sparrows under control, although they have been under attack for centuries. Probably the most obvious form of pest control is to pay some form of reward for their destruction. It was done very long ago for sparrows, and the money was handed out by the Parish Authorities through church wardens. In recent years there was a bonus on the tails of the grey squirrels – not paid by the Church. At last it is acknowledged that this method is almost useless if for no other reason than that the recipient of the reward is not likely to destroy the pest which is his income. Reduced numbers leads to the rapid breeding of survivors.

In passing mention should be made of the hedge sparrow which is very badly named. It is not a sparrow and does no harm. I have seen and heard them all in Wallace's Ground, although their rather weak little song is more common in the gardens of the valley. They do no damage and are often mistakenly regarded as female robins. This is not as silly as it sounds because their shape is not unlike a robins, and they live similar fairly solitary lives. Plenty of countrymen, with no interest in birds, are unaware of the fact that male and female robins have equally red breasts. We expect the male to be more decorative, possibly with pheasants in mind. A hedge sparrow differs no more from a robin than does, say, a female from a male blackbird.

Wallace's Ground on a fine summer evening has always wakened dreams in me – which is really not as contradictory as it sounds. As a boy I would lean on the west gate and look over the hills to the sunset. I was usually weary, sweaty and dusty. Like most people I enjoyed laughter and the challenge of human company, yet possibly with more need than some for occasional solitude. 'The thoughts of youth are long, long thoughts'. Away to the horizon there was no trace of human houses, and probably there never had been. This land seemed to stand apart from the fret of work and worry. Celts, Romans, Saxons, Danes and Normans had come and gone. I was 'the heir of all the ages', with no limit to what I might achieve.

That waking dream of youth was very different from the present certainty that I shall be one who has come and gone. Yet in the darkening, quiet, scented dusk there are no regrets, no bitterness, and no despair.

When rain drives through the gate there is less temptation to linger, and low clouds shorten the twilight. Few people have had their summer holidays by Midsummer Day and possibly only country people have any feeling of the best being past when the nights first become longer. It is early in the year to be pessimistic about winter, yet in some ways there are signs of change which will end in decay. In the hedges the deep green of the foliage lasts for many weeks, but begins to loose its freshness by the end of June.

In the hedges of the Field the story of being 'over the top' follows much the same lines as in the herbage and crops. Faults appear which were not obvious earlier, some are of commercial importance, whereas others are trivial. For instance, by July most sycamore leaves carry black blotches, which seem to do little harm. The sycamores in Wallace's Ground hedge grow as bushes and not as trees. The crab apples are also bushes on the hedge bank. In occasional seasons they are attacked by the caterpillars of the lackey moth in a very big way, and loose all their leaves before the end of July. These caterpillars are known to most people with an apple or pear tree in the garden, but they seldom do obvious harm. Their peculiarity is for the caterpillars to live under a sort of tent of white silk which looks something like a thick cobweb.

Just as the sycamore spot does little harm, whereas the lackey maggot may be serious, so it is with the pests and diseases of grass and crops. What they all share is the interference in the lush green of early summer, with a patchy appearance of growth. Weeds in July have also influenced the colour of the Field and the length of plants. Wild oats in barley are in ear and well above the crop. In pasture the odd dock or spear thistle will have been left by grazing animals to make a smooth sward look ragged. In addition, by late July the cows will have grazed the land on three or four occasions, and dropped a good deal of dung on it. Apparently they dislike grazing on herbage they have recently soiled, and avoid it. This in itself would leave an uneven surface, and it is made worse by the dung encouraging extra strong growth.

The avoidance of old dung patches must be connected with a sense of smell rather than by unpalatability. Cows graze at least as often by night as during the day, probably more in very hot weather. On cloudy, moonless nights they have no difficulty in avoiding soiled land. When horses grazed Wallace's Ground they left it more uneven than cows, because cows dropped dung anywhere, and horses sought out definite areas for the purpose. These patches might cover acres, and the horses did not graze them at all even when they had bitten the rest of the Field absolutely bare.

It all sounds quite natural, and although sheep are not so fussy about herbage they have soiled, they show a preference for clean land. Fortunately cattle eat perfectly well behind horses, and the whole preference seems to be largely a question of about three weeks. This doubles or trebles the number like most things in farming it is not as simple as it sounds.

The new system is of fertilising pasture several times per annum, and of letting the cows graze small areas in a rotation of about three weeks. This doubles or trebles the number of cows kept per acre, and thus increases the thickness of their droppings. Yet patchy grazing in Wallace's Ground is not more common than it used to be, indeed it is less noticeable. On some soils on neighbouring farms this is not the case, and rough grass had to be topped by the mower fairly frequently. Why this should be is a bit of a mystery. On the well drained, chalky soil of the Field it could be that three weeks in summer is long enough for the dung to decay, leaving no taint on the herbage.

Grass for grazing retains much of the lively green of early summer, although the shade of green never quite regains the lush darkness of May. Without much doubt modern methods are successful in producing more grass which is an extension of summer. With crops of corn there are more complications than the simple aim of getting more leafy growth. There must be strength of straw, freedom from diseases of leaf and grain, plus control of weeds.

The patchy sowing of weed killers and fertilisers has already been mentioned as a cause for streaks in the crop. By July the early green changes with the emergence of the ear, in fact this can happen before May is out with winter barley sown in autumn. The stem and ear will not change to harvest colours for weeks, but the deep green of the leaf blades has gone.

Uneven growth and colour changes due to weeds are not what they used to be. Unfortunately, however, the control of some weeds seems to have given more chance to others which once were not a pest. Or it may be that the use of fertilisers has made it possible to grow cereals too often, so that grassy weeds of the same family as the cereals have a greater chance of becoming a menace. In Wallace's Ground wild oats were unknown, and rough stalked meadow grass was never a weed, but was a grass we sometimes sowed in a mixture intended to last several years. Today they are ugly weeds, and no simple spraying programme is available.

Cereal diseases which show in summer had not been tackled by scientists from the spraying angle much before 1970. Previously the line of control was to breed varieties with some resistance to such diseases as mildew, rust and leaf blotch – sometimes called rhynchosporium. All are ugly as well as unprofitable, and about the best results were 'tolerant' rather than 'immune' varieties. Unfortunately tolerance was inclined to break down, or, in the case of rust, new varieties of the disease appeared.

Work on sprays had gone on feverishly for years, but it was not until 1970 that a material was marketed on a commercial scale which claims to control mildew in cereals. In future there seems to be every hope that leaf diseases of cereals may not disfigure Wallace's Ground, but it will be a year or two yet, and fairly certainly some new problem will arise.

Strength of straw has been mentioned as an essential for good cereal yields. This may change the appearance of Wallace's Ground in several ways. A spray can be used which checks the growth of straw, which gives a dwarf look to the crop in late summer. A period of rain and gales might flatten a clean, tall crop, and this would be more likely to happen if weeds were abundant. In both cases July would see the colour of the ears of grain mixed with the dark green of crippled straw or weeds. Later in August a spray might be used on laid barley or oats which would alter the look of the crop again. It is possible to kill and dry the mess of ears and greenery. This 'desiccation' makes combining much easier, and the grain and straw may be fed to animals within four days. At the time of writing it is not considered safe to desiccate barley for malting, or wheat for human consumption. New chemicals are passed by a Government Authority every few weeks, and I am quoting only those which I have seen in action. This mention of sprays is a chancy business, because not only are new chemicals numerous, but some trusted discoveries have a habit of coming under suspicion. An instance is D.D.T., which has undoubtedly saved countless human lives.

Leaning on the west gate of Wallace's Ground is peaceful enough as summer ends, but things have certainly not gone 'onward the same', not even the gate itself. This tubular metal affair is twelve feet wide, and although it can be leant upon there could be no comfort in sitting on it. The gate of my youth was only nine feet wide, but did not conform to the pattern of the old five-barred wooden gates of the South Country.

It was the custom for the landlords to supply gates and for tenants to erect them. Our landlord was Winchester College, and they must have bought their gates wholesale instead of from local carpenters. The outer frame was of wood, with the normal wooden cross pieces, but the inner bars were metal rods. This may have made them stronger, but I rather doubt it. Gates seldom failed at the bars, but usually at the head post.

The gate posts of those days were certainly not mass produced. They were eight feet long of solid oak and more than two feet of this was buried very firmly. This underground bit, or butt, was cut square. Putting up a completely new gateway was a highly skilled and laborious job for two men. They were lucky to finish by evening.

It may sound quite easy to dig two deep holes, drop in the posts, and ram flints firmly round them. This needs only a strong arm, but before doing too much ramming it is well to use a plumb line. These posts must be vertical. Next comes the driving in of the hooks from which the gate will hang, and here it is necessary to remember that the entrance may be on a slope. Precisely where these hooks are placed will determine how the gate will swing. We may have a preference for the gate to swing open when it is unlatched, but more commonly the aim is to have it swinging gently shut unless it is held open. From experience I know that it is possible to hang a gate which flies shut with a shattering bang. It is also easy to have the gate at a very queer angle when shut. The aim is to have it level and clearing the ground by about nine inches, but the head may drag in the earth, or be high enough in the air for a sheep to walk under.

I have never risen above the grade of assistant gate hanger, but even this has coloured my behaviour. 'Sitting on a fence in the moonlight' may be a suitable subject for a song, but I am almost glad that sitting on modern gates is almost impossible. Unless you sit near the hinges your weight is almost sure to be distorting the delicate hang of the gate. Similarly if you must climb over a gate, instead of opening it, always get over as near the hinges as possible.

Leaning on a gate is harmless and laudable.

Chapter Five

'All the leaves are Gold'

G. K. Chesterton felt the wonder and mystery of the year dying in splendour, although he was very much a Londoner. In Wallace's Ground some of the shrubs in the hedge change their leaf colour as early as the end of August, but, as with all the seasons, it is hard to give a date for autumn. Even the wild plants in the hedges and lane are not a bit consistent, and the crops come to harvest in almost every month of the year.

September 23rd is the Autumn Equinox, and September 29th is Michaelmas Day, when quarterly rents are due. In some respects Michaelmas is roughly the middle of autumn, or at least much nearer to it than Midsummer is the middle of summer. The flame of colour in the hedges is established by Michaelmas but leaf fall is another story. In 1969 there were leaves in plenty at the end of November, whereas most countrymen expect bare branches by Guy Fawkes day. In fact pheasant shooting, legal from October 1st starts in earnest in early November, because the trees are generally bare by then.

Fox hunting starts formally at the same time, although since August Wallace's Ground has seen the occasional rider on his way to a cubbing meet. The Field offers no cover for pheasants, and a fox would only be likely to lie there on the few occasions when the crop is kale.

Autumn can only be timed accurately by noting bird migration. Some at least seem to go according to the length of day rather than by any alteration in food, or by cold or warm days. For instance the swift first swoops over the Field in the first week of May, and is suddenly missed in the last week of July. The swallow on the other hand lingers until October 20th, and gathers in flocks for a day or two discussing, the journey, as if reluctant to go.

This timing of migration by day length only seems to apply to visitors who come to Dorset to nest. Bad weather in autumn or winter will have a big influence on hungry travellers. Wood pigeons move in from the north-east, and so do starlings. The pigeon is not welcome when the Field is cropped with kale or cabbage. They can do enormous damage by eating the leaves and, when red clover was widely grown for hay, they could destroy a crop in hungry weather. Still, pigeons are relatively harmless in Wallace's Ground, as compared with market gardens, or districts where peas are grown. Here they can be the equivalent of locusts.

Starlings in the Field have little more than a nuisance status. Sheep have no objection to starlings perching on their backs, and it may be that they do some good by picking out large parasites such as the sheep ked. Against this they soil the wool, and might encourage maggot attacks in early autumn. They can put out the sun in the evening when they arrive in a dense cloud and settle for a few minutes of noisy conversation. The hedges of the Field do not tempt them to remain for roosting. They go on after ten minutes or so to unite with other flocks in coppiced woodland. Here their weight and their dung can turn a pleasant covert into an indescribable stinking slum, with broken branches, and ruined shrubs. Our great cities know what starlings can do on high buildings but the nuisance is worse in the country.

It is significant that because starlings are a nuisance in towns there are quite a few people who would be prepared to have large numbers of them destroyed. At present this is not done and all that is permitted is that their roosts can be made uncomfortable for them in various ways. This merely moves them to other buildings, which seems singularly useless. My point is that there would be little objection by citizens to killing a bird which is a nuisance. In the cities, however, there would be a much greater outcry if we suggested killing pigeons on a wholesale scale. This in spite of the fact that the pigeon is a menace to human food.

I may have given the false impression that the wholesale killing of all birds is forbidden. This is not true of several pest and nuisance birds such as the pigeon and starling. The owner or occupier of Wallace's Ground may kill them or employ someone else to do so. The difficulty is that the methods of killing must be humane, and most of the cheap, old practices are forbidden. This is as it should be, but it limits the chance of reducing numbers to any significant extent. For instance there must be no snare, no bird lime, no poison bait, and not even stupefying bait. The latter has been permitted under licence against pigeons, but the cost is higher than for cartridges.

The only time a country man would waste a cartridge on a starling would not be in the Field, but if he happened to have any thatched buildings or houses. These birds are devils in thatch. They will bore round holes three inches in diameter into a newly thatched roof for nesting, or pull straws from the ridge for no obvious reason. They do not use the straw but drop it in a bored manner. 'Wasting a cartridge' is a fair description of killing a couple of starlings; others will take their place at once. Thatched roofs must be protected with wire netting, but today there are not even thatched hay stacks in Wallace's Ground, and thus the starlings are only a very mild nuisance.

They are naturally insect and grub eaters and will sometimes hunt flies like a swallow. Unfortunately the starling does not confine itself to insects, it now eats grain and fruit, although I do not think this was true in my boyhood. Possibly the change of diet was hastened by their learning in the winter to take bread, cheese and scraps of cake, and anything else put out for more lovable birds by housewives. I am not alone in having an unreasonable dislike for starlings, whilst admitting they do little harm. I admit that their curious song can be stimulating. It is a strange mixture of chuckling, whistling, and imitation of other birds. They are always in a hurry, always running in a cocky manner, always quarrelling, and always hungry.

Other wild birds are more welcome visitors to Wallace's Ground in autumn, and their plumage usually looks very sleek and smooth. In my youth I remember looking at the birds feeding on the abundant seeds of hedgerow plants, and wondering why at this season of abundance they were not breeding. It seemed strange that there should be a month or two when most birds were merely having a good time and growing fat. The answer can be partially found in the fact that this does not happen to pigeons. They breed till late into August, and although they lay right through spring and summer their best survival results are when there is ripe grain available.

Usually only two eggs are laid at a time, and many early nestlings die, but there is every chance of two being reared in late July, and two more in early September. It has been suggested that numbers could be reduced by systematically destroying nests in the last week in July, and again six weeks later. Unfortunately this does nothing about the invasion from Scotland and the North of Europe.

Pigeons feed their young on a thick, partly digested substance, regurgitated from their crops. Apparently this is best when grain is available, rather than when the parents are feeding on cabbage leaves or other green stuff. It is here that they differ from many species of birds which vary their diet from animal to vegetable. It is not uncommon for the young of other birds to be fed on animal material such as caterpillars, slugs and insects. In Wallace's Ground the tits in the hedges are the Blue, Coal and the Great Tit. They feed their young exclusively on insects and grubs, but will take bread crumbs from valley bird tables for themselves in winter, although they prefer cheese or fat. The blackbirds feed their young on worms and grubs, but are quite happy to change to fruit for their own consumption. It is this change of diet which partially accounts for adults enjoying a long autumn holiday. Insects are fewer, but grain and fruit are wastefully abundant.

What often happens is that after breeding the birds go through a moult, when flight and reactions are slow. They hide in the thick bushes and are silent. With the moult over they emerge looking extremely smart and spry, but they do not breed. Perhaps it is because there would not be time for the young to be big enough to be self-supporting before winter. The fact that the pigeon feeds its young on grain seeds, whereas the blackbird uses animal materials is only a partial answer. There are plenty of insects in early September although they will decrease rapidly after frost, whereas grain from crops and stubbles can be abundant until late October. Certainly it is not a question of there being no time to gather food for nestlings in daylight. The day length is just about the same in early April and early September.

In crisp autumn weather it is pleasant to see the birds with their feathers puffed out at dawn. Presumably this puffing out helps to insulate the body against cold air, but in autumn it increases the impression of sleek fatness. The birds are very alert and bright eyed. It is quite different in a long winter with air-frost, when they are clinging desperately to life. The feathers are puffed out, but the eyes hold fear, and the movements are not brisk.

I do not think that the birds and animals in Wallace's Ground have any foreboding when they rejoice in the abundant food of autumn. The ability to foresee evil seems to be confined to man. As I look over the first hoar frost I know what lies ahead, and if this is higher intelligence perhaps it is not to be envied. Autumn can be as pleasant and as beautiful as spring. Yet the easy platitude on a perfect October day is to say 'this will help the winter along'. Or the more pessimistic countrymen weightedly promulgates – 'We shall suffer for this later.' I doubt if there is any truth in the latter saying.

The wild animals of the Field are like the birds in facing winter with their coats in first-class condition. The history of Wallace's Ground, starting with permanent pasture, and continuing with a rotation of crops, would in itself change living conditions. In my lifetime, however, there have been other factors affecting wild animals. The most obvious has been myxomatosis in rabbits, which must have had an influence on the food supply of foxes, stoats and weasels. Yet Wallace's Ground has never gone to extremes. I do not remember a season when any animals were a serious pest.

Twenty years ago naturalists placed the rabbit as second only to the rat as a pest. It is significant that long before myxomatosis the official Ministry of Agriculture view discounted the value of the rabbit carcass as cheap meat, and recommended gassing in burrows, when naturally bodies were not recovered. Where rabbits have returned in any numbers this is still the official advice, in spite of a greatly increased market for pet food. Wallace's Ground was never really troubled by rabbits and it is difficult to imagine any future problem. Changes in farming would lower their hope of building up, since hedges are less wide. Yet some return had taken place by the summer of 1970.

The brown rat, said to be mammal pest number one, has had many more changes in environment. In my youth rats infested the old buildings in the next field to Wallace's Ground. Some stayed there all the year, but food must have become scarce when the cattle were moved out for grazing. In summer a considerable number of rats lived in the hedgerows. Before the grain ripened they had a wide variety of diets. Their climbing powers were well known on the rafters of buildings in winter, and this was turned to scaling bushes in spring. The brown rat has always robbed the nests of wild birds of eggs and fledglings. They are aggressive fighters and no ordinary parent bird would have any chance against them. In fact they have been known to kill hens, although this needs a word of explanation.

I have no memory of any rat setting out to kill a hen for food. Their slaughter of young birds and small rabbits has always been stealthy. It is quite a different story if they are cornered by an adult hen, or by a doe rabbit. My memory of seeing one of Mother's hens killed in Wallace's Ground was when a rat was robbing a stray nest, and the hen returned. The old phrase about humans behaving like 'cornered rats' is a very good bit of observed natural history.

By autumn grain is abundant in the field, and this is the season when the rat's life has been changed in recent years. For many years the sheaves of wheat or barley were built into stacks. Today the combine harvester cuts and threshes the grain, which is removed to a modern store, where real efforts have been made to make the storage bins rat proof.

We built our stacks to hold enough sheaves to give a full day's work for the old threshing machines. To save time in moving the machine it was usual to put the stacks in a row, with just enough room between them for the mechanism. Indeed we gathered the produce of several fields into a row of stacks, usually on a dry ridge to give easy transport of threshed corn downhill in the mud of winter. There was a distinct fire hazard about this relative crowding of stacks, and it was not a bit unusual for a man to sit leaning against a stack for lunch, and to light a pipe immediately afterwards. With shame I confess to having done it myself, but without disaster.

A stack of sheaves in Wallace's Ground was an ideal home for rats when they moved from the hedge banks in autumn. It was easy to bore holes between sheaves, the straw gave wonderful warmth, and they could eat the walls of their home. The number of rats in a stack could be scores before Christmas, and they spoiled at least as much corn as they ate.

The old threshing involved two men on the stack who threw sheaves into the flat top of the thresher. Here one man cut the string of the sheaf, and another opened the packed bundle to feed it smoothly into the maw of the thresher. Another man at ground level 'minded the bags', which meant that he changed sacks when they were full from the gush of grain pouring down a shute. Two other men built the threshed straw into a stack, as it was shaken into an elevator at the end of the process. This was seven, plus a boy, or some similar inferior worker, who had to rake the 'chaff' into a heap. Chaff was sometimes called 'dust' and consisted mainly of the glumes which had enclosed the grain in the ear. In the old days of threshers driven by steam engines there was another man who was in charge of the outfit, who got up steam in the dawn, and spent the rest of the day in fairly leisurely stoking and oiling.

My early autumn memories of Wallace's Ground was of threshing the corn from adjoining fields. The men throwing sheaves to the thresher started the day on the roof of the stack, tossing them down, and finished throwing the last ones up from the straw bedding on the soil. As they worked downwards the rats retreated to the bottom. They seldom made a dash for safety until the very end. After all they had enjoyed a quiet, comfortable life for months, until the noisy machine came, with eight or nine human enemies.

It all seems very long ago and far away. I was surprised that I described it all as normal practice in a book for boys written in 1952. Combine harvesters were certainly becoming familiar at that time, but Wallace's Ground had never seen one. I finished the chapter on threshing, with rats very much in mind, and with these words. 'Since the war there has been a very good law which makes it necessary for farmers to enclose their stacks in wire netting before starting to thresh.'

The idea of this Act was that there should be a complete slaughter when the last few layers of sheaves were reached, and the rats dashed in all directions. Without the retaining netting quite a lot got away, although the men did their best with pitchforks, and a good dog was a treasure. There is a fascination in watching a skilled terrier avoiding being bitten himself, and yet working at a wonderful speed. There is one pounce, a terrific shake, which kills at once, and in seconds another rat is taken. Only later does the dog go back to inspect his prey, and he is obviously very proud of himself.

In speaking of pests the countryman usually mentions rats and mice in one breath. This is a bit confusing because the hedge banks of Wallace's Ground in autumn are also home for voles, which are lumped with mice by most of us, without being considered separately. When it comes to different species it is as well to note that there is only one variety of rat in the Field. We are told that the black rat came to England during the Crusades, whereas the brown rat arrived much later, when overseas trade increased in the 1700s.

At first sight there seems to be some sort of comparison with the red and grey squirrels. The grey came to England in living memory, whereas the red is native. For some reason no red squirrels were found in most areas after about the beginning of the war, but the grey became extremely common. Actually the rat is not a parallel case. The black is still found in London and in large ports, but the brown is the pest of the countryside. I have never come across any evidence to show that black rats were in hedges and stacks before the brown invasion but it is highly probable that they were. Our forefathers certainly had trouble with rats and mice or they would not have invented 'staddle' stones. Wallace's Ground once had a set of these, but they are now decorations in various gardens.

Staddle stones were shaped like mushrooms. Wooden grannaries were built on them and sometimes they carried a rough plank floor on which a corn stack was erected. The idea was that rats could climb the stem of the mushroom, but could not get over the overhang of the circular stone top. It worked reasonably well, but meant that all stacks of corn had to be carried up three or four steps to the granary. This was avoided by unloading from the tail end of a wagon, but the steps were necessary to let a man get into the granary when he was not using a wagon. Rats could get up the steps and gnaw the wooden door, so the steps had to be hooked on, and readily removable.

Of the mice making an autumn migration from Wallace's Ground to adjacent sheds the worst pest is the house mouse. Like rats some of them stay out all the winter, and some stay in buildings all the summer. In the old buildings they consumed and fouled grain just like rats. New buildings are designed to keep them from the actual grain stores, but it is harder to stop invasion of many cattle sheds, and then a new danger arises. They will bite a hole in a lead water pipe, which is messy and annoying. What can be a disaster is a hole bitten in the insulation of an electric wire. This can start a fire.

At one time the old sheds in the field adjoining Wallace's Ground were occupied by semi-wild cats. We had a foreman who loved cats, and every day he scrounged several pints of milk for them. They were never fed solid food, but I am sure they were worth their milk. They killed hundreds of house mice and young rats, besides travelling several hundred yards to find half grown rabbits in hedges. Their numbers fluctuated and varied from two or three to at least thirty. Foreman tried to find homes for kittens in the village, but his supply exceeded demand. What caused the fluctuation was the usual natural cause of disease due to overcrowding. This certainly happened with rabbits long before myxomatosis.

A more pleasant species of mouse lives in the hedges of Wallace's Ground and does not migrate to the buildings in winter. It is the long-tailed field mouse, which is not greatly different in appearance from the house mouse. Probably I describe it as more pleasant, because it does not come to the buildings to cause obvious damage. Its food in the Field is corn, when this is available, and it eats berries and underground bulbs, which have no value to the farmer. In village gardens there is quite a different story, where bulbs and seed peas are important.

For at least twenty years I have not seen the smallest of all mice in Wallace's Ground. This was called the harvest mouse, and was so tiny that it could run up a stalk of wheat to get at the grain. Why it has vanished is a mystery, since no active steps have been taken against it, and it went well before the age of modern weed killers.

So much for the real mice of the Ground. I wrote that voles are 'lumped in' with them, and this is certainly true of the field vole. They do not come to the buildings in autumn, but they eat much the same food as the house mouse. They are responsible for one bit of damage not caused by mice. The long-tail mouse lives in holes but these are in the bank, and unimportant. The field vole makes a maze of burrows spreading out over the land. In autumn these can cause a combine harvester wheel to drop unexpectedly, and to dig the cutter into the stony earth. In addition the fact that the field vole is under the soil, out in the Field, means that it takes seed corn immediately after sowing. Mice and bank voles do not go many yards from the hedge bank and this headland is normally the worst crop in the Ground for other reasons. Implements have to turn on the headland and this compacts the soil. In addition weeds spread out from the hedge, and the shrubs of the hedge rob the adjacent soil.

The fox is only an autumn visitor to the Field when kale is grown, and it cannot be regarded as a pest. Mother certainly lost some birds in the very old days when hens were on free range. Our other commercial spell of poultry keeping, using fold units, was fox proof. In fact in these days, when most poultry are housed continuously, it is difficult to class the fox as a pest except at lambing time. If the modern fashion for lambing undercover should extend, as some people predict, the fox would not be a pest at all. This may be unlikely, but it is possible. At present the main fox diet, in the absence of rabbits, is mainly of vermin – mice, voles and rats. In addition he eats agriculturally unimportant meat such as frogs and ground nesting birds.

It is true that ground nesting birds includes partridges, but shooting is as much a blood sport as hunting. It would be ironic to find hunting condemned because – 'the fox is a harmless creature, of agricultural value in controlling rats and mice'. Incidentally, when Foreman had the old buildings and adjoining Wallace's Ground swarming with cats, I do not remember one being taken by a fox. Many country people fear attack by foxes on their pet cats, but I do not believe there is any truth in the belief that foxes love eating cats. I also think that most cats would 'see off' a single fox, and foxes are solitary hunters.

Perhaps it should be established that I am a cat lover, in an advanced state of unreasonable devotion. Foxes, on the other hand, are smelly, cruel, cunning, dirty in their homes, and kill for fun on a wholesale scale.

In autumn it is not uncommon to see some wild hunters who are not solitary. The weasel family are all ruthless killers, they have a sleek beauty, but with the devil in their eyes. We never see the pine martin or polecat in Wallace's Ground, although my Grandfather told me the polecat had been fairly common in his time. These big weasels were obvious enemies of the shooting squire at one end of the social structure, and of the humble rabbit trapper at the other. Stoats and weasels are disliked by keepers, but did little obvious harm to the rabbit trappers, which may account for their survival in fair numbers. Stoats killed and ate rabbits, but did not raid the trapper's night catch on a wholesale scale.

I have seen tiny weasels crossing the lane by Wallace's Ground in single file, but I do not think they were hunting. The mother seldom sticks to one resting spot for many days, presumably for safety reasons. When they are young she transports her offspring one by one in her mouth, later they follow her nose-to-tail. On the other hand I have seen stoats follow a rabbit in the Field. They went very fast in single file, and were not diverted by other rabbits who got up near them. I have no doubt their quarry was doomed, because his hole would be no obstacle to the stoats. In a strange way the rabbit moved stiffly, but he was well in front. There could not have been any question of the power in the eye of the stoat which is said to mesmerise a rabbit. On the other hand I could see no advantage to the stoats in hunting in single file. It was certainly not the 'pack' method used by wolves. Probably it was merely a parent teaching her family their bloody trade, and the slow rabbit was too frightened to move freely.

Of all the wild animals in the Field the hedgehog is the only one which really hibernates. By Autumn he will have found a hollow in the slight ditch by the hedge bank, which is full of straw or dried leaves, and there he will start that strange suspension of life which is so desirable in an English winter. In other ways he is the strangest of the large creatures in this little world of the Field. He makes a great deal of noise, grunting as he walks in the evening. His flesh is very palatable and he has only one means of defence. He can neither run fast, nor bite, nor kick. All he can do is to roll in a ball, which presents a sphere of prickles to foxes and badgers. This is singularly useless against approaching tractor wheels, and some foxes and badgers have discovered ways to make him uncurl. Once the following was my feeling about hedgehogs:

> 'It is surprising that the hedgehog has survived, not only because of predators, but because of

human activity. This strange creature attracted many legends to himself in the days of witchcraft, and witches lasted well into my young manhood. It might still be possible to find aged countrymen who believe that hedgehogs suck the milk of cows at night. Well, they will drink milk readily from a saucer, but their mouths simply could not deal with a cow's teat. They are accused of taking hen's eggs by impaling them on the prickles of their backs. Again they like raw egg in a saucer, but the spines on their bodies simply will not fit the carrying story. In fact as an eater of slugs, maggots, caterpillars and grubs the hedgehog is the farmer's friend, and has been grossly libelled.'

The previous paragraph was written by me in 1947 for the script of our broadcast, 'A Field in Dorset', mentioned in Chapter One. At that time I think it was the reaction of every naturalist. In 1970 an old friend, Dr Maurice Burton, had some very different things to say about hedgehogs on the radio. He described how a research worker had left a bottle of milk within reach of a hedgehog. The bottle was fitted with the sort of rubber teat which is used on farms for suckling calves. The hedgehog immediately sucked the teat, and emptied the bottle, doing some damage to the rubber in the process. Dr Burton went on to say that a number of vets have described the wounding of cow's teats, and blamed it on hedgehogs. This damage occurs only in relatively warm weather and not in winter when they are hibernating. Finally he confirmed that hedgehogs can pick up apples on their spines, but made no mention of carrying hen's eggs.

In Wallace's Ground I have seen hedgehogs scuttle away from a cow lying on the turf, but have never seen one sucking the teats. On the whole I am not completely convinced that I was mistaken in my old idea that sucking does not take place. The artificial teat used for calf rearing is distinctly smaller than that of most cows. The veterinary evidence is not conclusive, in that it deals with injury rather than observed suckling.

My own theory is based on the fact that hedgehogs do like milk, and that a little is sometimes squeezed from the udder of a high yielding cow in the process of lying down. The hedgehog licks this milk from the outside of the udder, and in continuing to lick may damage the teat. It is true that hedgehogs standing on their hind legs could reach the udders of many cows, and could suck without the cow needing to lie down. This does not rule out my theory, because as the time for early morning milking approaches a heavy yielder may well leak a little milk in the standing position.

As for carrying hen's eggs stuck on their spines, I am not satisfied that this is true merely because it has been observed with apples. There is a considerable difference between eggs and apples. To my mind a hedgehog would eat an egg on the spot, and would break it if it tried rolling on it for transport. The apples were probably picked up quite accidentally in rolling for fun. What the modern scientific investigation does prove is that our fathers were not fools inventing wild legends about hedgehogs. Gamekeepers have some justification in blaming these creatures for eating the eggs of ground nesting game, but this is not my concern in Wallace's Ground.

The skin of the hedgehog cannot be described as sleek at any season, but the word applies to most other wild animals and birds in autumn. It certainly described the coat of the tame sheep and cattle in the Field.

Of the less common wild creatures I once saw a fallow deer in October in Wallace's Ground. I cannot vouch for the autumnal condition of its coat, because my inspection was brief. There was a strong wind in my face as I came up the lane early in the morning. This hid the sound of my footsteps and blew my scent away from the Field. There were young heifers in the Field, and on arriving at the gate I gave them the usual countryman's inspection. This involves counting to make sure none had strayed, and I suddenly realised there was one too many. It was over in seconds, the animals looked up from grazing, and the extra 'heifer' took a standing leap-off yards away from me, and was over the far hedge before I knew what had happened.

It was a fallow deer and one of the very few I have seen wild in daylight. It is not unusual to see a herd cross the road in car headlamps, and some Dorset farmers have suffered serious damage to corn crops. There are plenty in my district, but never far from woodland, and Wallace's Ground is on a bare chalk plateau. Heaven knows what had happened to separate this one hind from the herd. Possibly in the night a car headlamp had frightened this one deer to turn back, when it was the last of a string crossing a lonely road. Deer have a fairly strong flocking instinct, and panic can set in when one finds itself alone, with no knowledge of the whereabouts of its fellows.

The flocking necessity is not as strong with fallow deer as with sheep, but I once came across the panic effect of sudden solitude on sheep. We were driving sheep along the lane into Wallace's Ground when an impatient young dog cut the last sheep from the flock and drove it a score of yards down the lane. An older dog would have passed the stray and brought it back, but I probably swore at the wrong moment, and the youngster came to heel with every sign of penitence. By then the sheep was well out of sight or sound of her fellows, and seemed to go mad. She ran straight on down hill, across a road, up a lane and then over gates and hedges on our neighbour's farm. We found her hours later, two miles away, grazing quietly with our neighbour's flock.

I think something similar to this had happened to my solitary deer in the Field. I have come across similar panic in a single fallow deer, who ran into the side of my car in broad daylight. It seemed to be running without looking straight ahead, which is usually confined to the hare. In fact the setting of the eyes in the hare prevent it seeing straight ahead, which is not the case with the deer.

One common animal we never get in Wallace's Ground is the mole, and this is a cause for satisfaction. The reason is partly the shallow soil, but this would provide a reasonable living for them in summer. The mole lives very largely on earthworms, and the Field contains its share of these. The main cause of the absence of these fascinating little mammals is that in winter we may get a frost which prevents burrowing over the full depth of the soil. Moles can be plentiful in soils which are just as shallow as the chalk, but in these cases it is usual to find woodland adjoining. Indeed there are plenty in chalk fields which adjoin coppices. Apparently the moles spend the winter in the coppice or shrub land where there is a soil-cover of leafmould, which stops freezing, and keeps the worms near the surface. Then in the spring they move out into nearby pasture or cultivated land. Wallace's Ground has no woods or coppice within at least half a mile.

My satisfaction at the absence of moles is due to the fact that mole hills can interfere with grass mowers and the knives of combine harvesters. The little mounds of earth also cover some grazing, and dislodge the roots of crops. This is only serious in valuable market garden crops, and all moles would do in the Field is the mechanical damage to machinery previously mentioned.

On second thoughts it might be right to regard moles as a pest because they feed mainly on earthworms, and they have an insatiable appetite. We used to be taught that moles will die if they do not eat every hour, but this may be an exaggeration. It is fairly certain that although they eat pests such as wireworm in the soil, the earthworm is their favourite. Darwin taught that earthworms are closely connected with soil formation. They loosen and aerate the top layer right into the subsoil. They also draw in fallen leaves and other vegetation, which they eat together with large quantities of soil. He estimated that ten tons of soil per acre passed through their bodies every year, which is rendered friable and mixed with rotting vegetation. In spite of this I have only met one Dorset farmer who was concerned about the increased number of seagulls following the plough and eating worms. Most of us remember vaguely that worms are good but do nothing about it.

There was once some advertising from a man or firm which would supply earthworms to increase soil fertility. I have heard nothing of this recently, and presumably few farms are totally lacking in worms. They increase very rapidly in favourable conditions, such as generous applications of dung. There are probably plenty for the birds and the moles, especially where farming is good..

Never having had moles in Wallace's Ground my youth was lacking in one source of pocket money. Trapping moles was a highly skilled job, and their skins were valuable. Today, if they are a nuisance, the usual procedure is to poison them with strychnine; the old mole catchers died out with the rabbit trappers. Poisoning in their burrows means that no bodies are recovered for skinning.

When Wallace's Ground is in grass the autumn is a time when food is very abundant for the sheep and cattle. At least this is true of late autumn, although very occasionally a summer drought may last into September. This suits the rest of the farm where my nephew is first concerned with grain harvest, and then with stirring the stubbles before the soil gets too wet. Very seldom is a summer drought followed immediately by hard frost. Winter does not often come in one step, but we expect a period of rain to be swept in by fairly warm westerly gales. Clay soils become so wet quickly that cattle must be removed, but this does not happen to the Field. Grass continues to grow in October, and only the gate-ways are muddy. The danger in farming is over-valuing this autumn grass. The huge paunches of cows and ewes need filling with some bulky food and autumn grass supplies the necessary fibre, but that is about all. The feeding value for milk production is low, and in Wallace's Ground cows and sheep are expected to provide high milk yields in winter.

This is clean against nature and must be accepted as such. The growing grass on this dry hill field will make it possible to postpone the feeding of hay and silage, but there must be no economy on modern protein foods. This is a season when good farmers are tempted to be slow in giving too little purchased cattle food. Yet at no other time is it so dangerous to under-feed. If the milk yield drops in October the best that lavish feeding can then do is to hold it at the lower level.

Possibly the reason for mistakes being common is that winter milk production used to be confined to the immediate neighbourhood of big towns. Cows were kept in city cellars until the railways made it possible to transport churns from a radius of about 80 miles of London. Lorry networks came much later, and real distant transport was only useful after pasteurisation had made milk keep. One addition at the beginning of the century, when I first knew Wallace's Ground, the compounding of animal feeding stuffs was a small, and rather crude trade. It is only in the last 25 years that it has become a giant industry, measured in hundreds of million £s.

There is a farming tradition working against purchased foods which must still have a faint influence on the minds of men brought up on the farms of the first half of this century. There is also the fact that changes in the supply and demand for milk is still altering. I wrote of autumn grass in Wallace's Ground needing a supplement for cows of high protein food in order to avoid a fall in milk yield. This is only true because the Field is managed as part of a farm which accepts the 1960–70 need for a constant supply of milk throughout the year. This may well change before 1980, and there are farmers in the south-west who are changing to the more natural system of calving in spring. Long-keeping milk already exists, and problems of the cost of processing may soon be solved.

Looking at cows in Wallace's Ground will not change; they will still be grazing controlled strips of grass in spring, summer and autumn. In winter they will be housed, and the date of calving will merely have changed back to the custom of our fathers, before there was a cattle cake industry. In fact the food compounder will still exist without much demand from cows. Poultry and pigs seem firmly committed to an indoor system, and eggs, poultry meat, pork and bacon are all increasing in Britain. Only with cows is there a trend to more grazing and less artificial feeding.

What concerns me a little is that only countrymen will appreciate the difficulty behind changing from all-the-year calving to the natural dates of February to mid-April. Perhaps using the word 'natural' gives the impression that it will be quick and easy. Cows carry their calves for 40–41 weeks, so that if a calf is desired on February 25th successful mating should take place on May 20th. The farmer aims at having his cows calving on about the same date every year, because this gives them a rest of about 8 weeks from the time they cease yielding milk to the time when they start afresh. This is likely to work well with February 25th calves, because when they were mated on May 20th they had been enjoying several weeks of plentiful grazing. Cows calving on September 7th on the other hand were mated on November 6th, when grass had possessed little feeding value for some time. Mating when a cow is going back in condition may not succeed, and an autumn calving herd tends to take more than a year between calving dates.

This explains why an all-the-year calving dairy tends to slip towards spring breeding, but it is not much help in suggesting how a farmer can deliberately make the change quickly and cheaply. The cow which should have been mated on November 6th would have to be kept till May 20th producing nothing, if the change was to be done in one year. Half the herd would be absolutely useless for six months.

A young farmer, living three ridges of rolling country east from Wallace's Ground, is seeking to establish a spring calving dairy by starting with heifers. This sounds easy, and it would be if he sold his older cows at a high price when they calve in autumn, and bought heifers freshly calved in spring. Unfortunately this involves going to market for his heifers, and losing the advantages of home breeding. Such advantages are more than might appear at first sight. Every farmer likes the animals he has bred and reared for what may seem sentimental reasons. His neighbours may think rightly that his line of blood has nothing very outstanding to recommend it. There is, however, a reason for home rearing which may be more important than pedigree. The young receive from their mothers a degree of protection from certain diseases. The strains of disease organisms differ from farm to farm, and home-bred livestock often have a resistance which is lacking in animals from a distance. This is additional to the stress which is inevitable in travel, and in the conditions of an auction.

To get a start quickly, and to avoid market purchase our neighbour has to think of the age at which he will first mate his heifers. Obviously if a cow had calved on September 6th, 1968 and her daughter was required to breed at the same date in 1971 she would be mated about November 6th, 1970, at the age of 2 years and 2 months. On the other hand if the heifers were to be all calved in spring then mating would be 8 months earlier when the heifer might not be fully grown. Heifers mated before they are well developed are often stunted for the rest of their milking lives.

In suggesting a heifer would normally be expected to calve at 3 years of age I am referring to a September born calf of one of the larger breeds, such as the Friesian. A Jersey could be expected to reproduce at 2 years, and the modern generous feeding of heifers has reduced my old-fashioned ages. A well reared Friesian might well be mated to calve at about 2 years old, but this is no help if we want a heifer born in September to calve in late February, she must be too young or wastefully old.

What our neighbour is doing in establishing his spring calving herd is mating his autumn born females well before I would have advised. So far, at the end of their first summer, they have milked well, but they are a little below normal size. There is a real problem to be solved if Wallace's Ground carries a herd which all calve in spring. Returning to a natural date takes more time than an outsider might imagine. This is one of the adjustments which might be necessary if we join the Common Market. The suggested 3 years to modify British conditions sounds simple, but the countryman knows it is desperately short.

Autumn sheep in Wallace's Ground are one of the things which take the sadness out of autumn. Almost all breeds mate in November to lamb in April. This is comforting in much the same way that buds and seeds speak of the certainty of new life after winter death. The local breed, the Dorset Horn, go a lot further. They lamb in October, and there is new life abounding in the Field, in the darkest of the shortening days.

All breeds of sheep look at their best in autumn, when their new fleece is fully grown, and before it has a chance to become tattered. A Dorset Horn lamb has a touch of the miraculous in the extreme whiteness of its wool, and the lack of any trace of black in the hair of legs or face. The lamb has always been a symbol of helpless innocence, and the shining white of this breed is the nearest thing I know to perfection. They are utterly fearless, like many young animals, wild or tame. In brief autumn sunlight they play complicated games of 'king of the castle' if someone has dropped a bale of hay, or there is any slight mound of earth. There is much leaping, dancing sideways, and butting with a sudden pause at any moment to dash back to mother for a sup of milk. There is no greater expression of ecstasy than the quivering of a lamb's tail as he sucks.

As I watch young lambs in Wallace's Ground my thoughts go back to boyhood when I used to be detailed to help shepherd. On the whole it meant carrying hurdles for him and doing the heavier bits of toil. Still he taught me quite a bit of his craft, and I know the loneliness of an autumn night in the lambing pen. There was a glow of pride in the cold dawn when I had not lost a lamb nor a ewe, and could greet my Father with a satisfactory report.

Generally ewes lamb without trouble, and do not need attention. Most shepherds like to be present, to clear any mucus from the mouth, to blow down the new arrival's throat and to make sure that the mother 'takes to it'. The blowing is the old equivalent of the 'kiss of life' presumably, but is usually only a bit of routine. Seeing the ewe 'taking to it' is more important. With a single lamb the mother licks it vigorously all over, and within a few minutes the lamb has staggered to its feet. In a strange blundering way its instinct guides it to search along mum's body for the udder. It makes several attempts to seize a teat, and then all is well. The joyful quivering of the tail heralds an amazingly quick build-up of strength. The helpless newly born can be jumping and running in 12 hours.

What might go wrong? Quite a lot, such as the ewe having a sore udder or teats, which will lead her, against her will, to butt her own lamb away. Shepherd has usually spotted this before lambing and effected a cure, or he may have to foster the newly born on another freshly lambed ewe.

A much more common difficulty is that if the ewe has twins, labour may start with the second before the first has been cleaned. In fact as the second labour starts the ewe may walk a few steps away from the helpless first born. This will give a fox just the chance he likes, apart from the fact that the separated lamb may be abandoned. With the shepherd present the first born will not be lost, and it will suffer no harm if it does not get its first meal until several hours after birth.

I realised the last fact when we had a few lambs being born in the Field in January which is very late for Dorset Horns. The weather was bitterly cold, and the newly born lambs were literally freezing on the grass before they could be licked dry. I got over this by covering the lambs with hay until daylight brought a little heat, and I could be sure their mothers looked after them. I learnt this trick from watching a Hampshire Down shepherd, whose flock always lambed in January. In bitter weather, when lambs were coming fast, he always kept a mound of loose straw in the lambing pen. As soon as a lamb arrived during the night he was pushed into the heap of straw with only his head sticking out. No one who had seen it could forget that pile of straw dotted with small black heads. Actually the white faces of our own sheep would have looked prettier, if less fantastic, but fortunately most of my lambing experience in Wallace's Ground was in the milder autumn nights of October.

Fostering lambs on ewes happens every year in every flock. Sometimes a neighbour will have a spare lamb or two with no mother capable of taking them. Sometimes the reverse is true and we have ewes with a super-abundance of milk and no spare lamb. The telephone has helped a great deal in swapping lambs between flocks. In my youth it often meant a long ride on horseback, to tour a radius of a few miles in the hope of finding, or getting rid of very young lambs. We frequently reared four or five on cows' milk from a bottle. These 'pet' lambs were very charming when young and playmates for children. Unfortunately lambs grow much faster than children and in a few weeks a pleasant companion could become a butting menace. These pet lambs seldom grew as fast as those suckling their mothers, and I am doubtful if it would pay to rear them by paid workers. Fortunately there is usually a wife, or a sister of the farmer to provide unpaid labour at most inconvenient hours.

Fostering on another sheep has its difficulties. It seems certain that ewes recognise their own lambs by their smell. Lambs recognise their mothers in the same way, but they are not at all fussy about joining any ewe which will permit them to suck. What the shepherd has to get over in fostering is the stern refusal of the ewe to accept any lamb except her own. The traditional method is to skin the dead lamb and to tie this skin over the youngster which we want the bereaved ewe to take. The substitute is alleged to smell like its predecessor, and the skin is left on for several days.

It is a strange sight to see little lambs wandering about in a tattered skin coat, which soon begins to stink. I was taught this bit of shepherding in Wallace's Ground, and can remember the skinning as a messy job. I never had very much luck with it, and certainly never found the ewe to be completely deceived. It was far easier, and cleaner, to put the ewe in a very small pen, with head fastened in a forked pole. She could eat, but could not turn round to smell the new lamb, and was quite unable to butt it away. At first she tended to kick at it, but the pressure of milk in her udder soon persuaded her to allow suckling. It might be necessary to keep ewes in this close control for at least a couple of days before the alien lamb was completely accepted.

I have heard that sprays are available which act as deodorants, or which attract the ewe to the foster lamb, but they were after my time, and I have no personal experience. It is an autumnal experience to watch the young lambs in Wallace's Ground, and to realise that I have come to autumn like the year. Time was, when I was a young science student, and professional jobs were difficult to find. I looked over this same view from the Field, and comforted myself that I could always get a job as a shepherd.

It is unpleasant to realise that my autumn has made me incapable of the toil involved. I could not hold a sheep to pare its hooves against footrot, nor get down to help in a difficult lambing. No one would employ me as a shepherd. What is comforting is that good shepherds at fairs still talk to me as an equal in the craft. They tell me things without explaining, because we speak the same language.

When Wallace's Ground is in crops the timing of autumn is wildly varied, and more so than it was a generation ago. There were always seasons when the crops ripened earlier or later according to the weather in July and August, but the variety of crops were reasonably established. Today there are strong reasons for using breeds of wheat and barley which will 'spread' the harvest. Instead of gangs of men we now have expensive machines which have only one use – to cut and thresh cereals. If the corn all ripened together we should need two machines, each working for only about three weeks in the year. For all the rest of the time they would represent great chunks of locked-up money. Hence the aim is to get some varieties of corn maturing early, and some late, so that one machine can be at work for, say, six weeks.

This need was less urgent with our fathers, and they had no great choice of breeds. Spring sown barley ripened later than autumn sown varieties, but then the autumn barleys were less valuable. Spring wheat yielded less than winter sown wheat, whereas winter oats were generally less reliable than spring. Plant breeders were at work, but without any strong incentive because of a curious weakness of law.

It is fortunate that the modern need for a spread harvest coincided with a change in the laws of what could be called 'copyright' in plant production. Not long ago the plant breeder had no right to royalties on anything he produced. He could only collect anything from his labours by keeping all the grain in his own hands until he had multiplied it to a large tonnage. Then he could sell at a high price for the one year – always assuming he could find purchasers. After the first sale he received no reward.

A good deal of plant breeding was confined to Research Stations, but some was done by a few commercial firms, with a high reputation. On the other hand a number of equally good seed firms publicly stated that they did no breeding. They claimed to sell good clean seed, correctly named, but with nothing in the way of crossing or selection. There also existed a certain amount of renaming varieties bred by scientists, and selling them at fancy prices, which was obviously dishonest.

Now that breeders are protected, and encouraged by royalties, there are signs of considerable progress. In 1970 I saw winter barley, of excellent yield, harvested on July 12th. This spread the use of my neighbour's combine harvester by 15 days, beyond anything he had ever managed before. It seems that Wallace's Ground in future will be showing the colours of harvest at any time between the end of June and the end of August. If the colours remain much after the end of August it will be because rain has stopped the machines. On average the stubble will probably be bare by mid-September, but October harvesting is a sad job which can happen in a wet year even with the latest machines.

Autumn and corn harvest may have to be separated in our thoughts, now that winter barley may be ripe a fortnight after Midsummer Day. Ripe wheat and August still come together, and my best memories of Wallace's Ground in autumn are of a level wheat crop ready for the combine harvester. Yet I know that the sight of those heavy ears has lost most of its meaning for a younger generation. Wheat is not the 'staff of life', and the word 'bread' no longer means 'food' as it does in: 'Give us this day our daily bread.' For that matter English wheat does not make the sort of bread which has been popular in England for more than half a century. It would make excellent French rolls, and you may claim to enjoy bread by the yard. Yet a roll must be eaten straight from the oven, whereas, whatever they may claim, the English continue to eat their bread and butter sliced thinly from yesterday's loaf. This is varied by preferring yesterday's loaf supplied ready sliced.

Hymns have joined prayers in losing some of their meaning. 'They shall come rejoicing bringing in the sheaves,' is a folk song which has become a hymn. There has been no sheaf in Wallace's Ground, none on the farm, and none in the village for at least a dozen years. One giant machine now crawls round the Field, leaving rows of shining loose straw behind it. The grain will be sold, and most of it will be compounded into pig, poultry and cattle foods.

All our civilisation hung on the autumn harvest and it is curious how the influence remains, when there is no longer any justification for it. The long vacation originated so that all scholars could work in the harvest fields. Today only 3 per cent of the English population is directly connected with farming, and corn farming does not interest a very large percentage of these few. Even on corn farms there is no longer a powerful need to bring the young home to work in August and early September.

In my own youth there was no question about how I should spend the long summer holiday. My only hope of getting to the seaside was if the weather was exceptionally kind, and we finished harvest before school or college reopened. Even when I had started work outside farming it was taken for granted that I would take my annual leave in August and come home to work with the sheaves. Recently on the radio a farmer in late July said that now harvest had started he was taking his wife for three weeks holiday in Spain. The argument seemed to be that corn harvest is so highly mechanised that it can be left to the skilled farm workers of today. He is certainly right, but it would be dead against my own instincts to be far away from Wallace's Ground at harvest time, even although I have no financial connection with the farm. Ripe grain draws me back to the farm in autumn, and especially if this Field is in corn.

The radio farmer just quoted had realised a new twist in farming. Harvest is obviously important, and is a first priority, but in many ways it is scientifically controlled. The grain as it comes from the combine is tested for moisture. The man in charge of drying and storage has facts to guide him in the use of the machines in his care. Experience and judgement have remained much more important in connection with cultivations. Possibly it is vital that the farmer should be at home when the stubbles are cleared. No meter helps in deciding if the soil should be ploughed, or stirred with rotating blades, or sliced with disc harrows. All are agreed that movement is necessary for weed control at the earliest possible moment after grain and straw have been removed. I have seen the cultivators in Wallace's Ground at the same time as the straw baler.

In a way this new urgency takes some of the colour out of autumn. In October stubbles were covered in early morning with millions of spiders' webs each coated with dew, and making rainbows in the first light of the sun. At that season the rays sweep low over the Field from the further hills. As the dew dries the webs seem to disappear, but they still coat your boots with gossamer at noon, although your eyes cannot see the individual strands.

The fantastic number of these spiders is hard to believe. The sun on the dew-coated web has a similar influence on the human mind as looking through a microscope at a drop of soil water. Both bring a realisation of the fantastic number of living creatures in our world. Wallace's Ground in autumn intensifies the feeling I had when we wrote the radio script in 1947. One field in Dorset is too big for understanding. It means 'home' to me but I shall never know all its possibilities. Without attempting to describe any deep spiritual influence it may have had on me, it is sufficient to say that I am surprised every year by the way harvest abundance merges into winter sleep.

Here in Dorset there is seldom any spectacular end to autumn. In October a still sunny day may be followed by a clear night. It means a frost which is enough to kill the runner beans in the valley, but it makes very little obvious difference to the Field. The grass stops growing when the land is in pasture, but it is very seldom hard enough to freeze the soil if the rotation has brought stubble cultivation. Almost the only constant thing about autumn is that night frost in October, and I can only remember one year when there was no killing cold before late November.

Actually the common experience of autumn is rain, and those still sunny days and crisp nights are pleasant. More usually on the hill, the setting sun across the valley finds no more than a thin patch in the scudding cloud. The light passes and all colours suddenly become grey. It was in Wallace's Ground that I first realised how suddenly colour vanishes with the coming of darkness, even with a bright Harvest Moon.

After a dry harvest the first autumn rain gives an acrid smell on the dusty earth. As it falls harder every soil grain swells a little as it absorbs water. Soon the surface is saturated and the wet soaks in deeper and deeper, through the soil to the porous chalk beneath. No one has ever dug a well in Wallace's Ground, but I have known it done in similar circumstances. Almost certainly there is about 300 feet of thirsty chalk under the few inches of top soil. The water is filtered through this massive depth before it reaches impervious clay. There a tilt in the strata may allow it to come to the surface again as a spring.

When the Dorset Horn sheep are in the middle of their unnatural October lambing it is essential for the shepherd to have some form of shelter. Usually this is a large hut on wheels with a stove in the corner. The hut smells sweetly of cattle cake, and there is room to stretch out on a few dry sacks over loose straw. However fast the lambs are coming there is usually a pause when no birth is imminent, and it is possible to lie down for an hour in the warmth, with the rain lashing on the roof. Old shepherd could take a nap and be certain to wake as he willed after 30 minutes or so. I could never trust myself. I would have slept for many hours, and all I dare do was lie there and think. There is a sort of bodily relaxation, which is a real rest, even with the brain working overtime.

The sound of the wind and rain often took my thoughts as a youth to the great filter of white chalk beneath the hill, and to the wonderful water from deep springs in the valley. I wonder what my present reactions would be to lying in stuffy warmth, although in garments soaked in patches. What would I think about in my own autumn, with insistent heavy rain falling, millions of drops, incessantly falling through the night?

Life slows up in autumn. So much is dying, so much now comes to a standstill, dormant, waiting. The butterfly pupa lies still and apparently lifeless, with no hint of the spring transformation. In the hedge banks the stems of the grasses are withered, but food has been passed down and stored in the roots. Next year's leaves are already there folded tightly in embryonic buds. The seed pods of weeds have split, so that a hundred thousand lie on the ground waiting for next year's damp and warmth. On a lambing night in Wallace's Ground I once worked out that 2 lb. of seed, carefully spread, would be enough to grow a thick crop of the weed charlock. Yet if it got out of hand several hundredweights would be produced per acre.

In the old days, before effective weed killers, charlock did sometimes get out of hand and seed. In one such failure of good husbandry the earth in autumn received a massive amount of seed. Charlock can live dormant in the soil for many years until it gets the precise conditions it likes for growth. Wallace's Ground was in pasture for at least 50 years, and the charlock seed just waited. The weed does not grow in firm grassland, but it came up thickly on the very first year the Field was ploughed.

To my nephew charlock is no longer a problem, but wild oats are more difficult to control with weed killers, and they can lie dormant to some extent. There is never any final answer to the curse of Eden, which forecast weeds and toil.

Wallace's Ground is an ordinary field at any time of the year. At the end of autumn it holds little attraction for the stranger. There is little colour in the leafless hedges, and the scents of spring and summer have gone with the white violets, the honeysuckle and sweet briar. The sight of distant fields is drab and grey, although there is one pleasant advantage for my sense of vision. With no foliage in the way it is easier to appreciate the great smooth curves of the horizon. There is also an intensification of the feeling of being blessedly alone.

Eric Shipton, the great mountaineer, spent a lifetime seeking what he describes as 'the Untravelled World'. He could enjoy good food, good drink and good company, but always returned to his need for solitude, preferably in unexplored places. Wallace's Ground is far from unexplored. It was made by man, yet it is possible to find solitude there. This is especially true on a late autumn evening at the week-end. There is nothing to tempt our occasional visitors to climb the hill. The cultivation of the farm has no great urgency about it, or at least not sufficient to pay overtime to tractor drivers. The care of livestock goes on, but the cows are housed, day and night, in the valley. Only in rare years of the rotation are sheep likely to be in the Field, and their presence is not disturbing. The lambing season is well over, and shepherd no longer spends long hours of day and night with them. The provision for hauling by tractor their rations of hay and cake was done in advance of Friday. There may be a little baaing by strayed lambs and anxious mothers.

The only other sound is the slow clank of half-a-dozen sheep bells, hanging from the necks of the six best looking ewes in the flock. This is peaceful and pleasant under most conditions, and quickens to a joyful peel when shepherd appears with food, and the sheep trot to meet him. Only very occasionally is there a wild jangling clamour which means that something is wrong. It may be that the sheep have broken through a fence, or they have been frightened into a panic by a dog.

I like the quiet of late autumn in the Field, especially at sunset. It sets me thinking of all the country people who have influenced me through Wallace's Ground.

Chapter Six

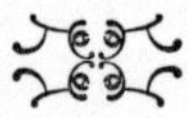

'People in the Field'

I always thought of Wallace's Ground as Mother's Field. Grandfather had been the first Wightman to be the occupier of the land, about a century ago, and he passed the tenancy over to my parents when they got married in 1881. At that time they had a butchers' shop and farmed about 60 acres of chalky soil. I was the youngest member of the family, born in 1901. By the time I was 10 years old, the farm had been expanded to about 500 acres, but I doubt if Mother had much idea of our boundaries, or had ever seen the more distant fields.

Her generation found plenty of exercise in work, and her walks for pleasure were confined to Sunday evenings in summer, after church. It was a stiff climb for a quarter of a mile up the farm lane, but it was worth it, and it was the only time she strolled for relaxation. There were other visits to the Field, but these were all connected with catering. It was one of the few fields in the neighbourhood with a reputation for mushrooms, but Mother seldom attempted to gather these. All the people in the village seemed to hear of the arrival of mushrooms within twenty-four hours, and the only hope of getting any was in the first light of dawn.

It was usually my job to wander about in the dew with wet feet, and I doubt if mushrooms with the breakfast bacon were worth it. Mother welcomed the tiniest buttons, not for immediate cooking, but for preserving in vinegar. There were two legends we all believed explicitly in those early days. The first was that mushrooms should be eaten or pickled on the day they were picked. This is quite untrue, but it may be a fact that any maggots will become more easily visible if they are kept. Actually if the stem is sliced, and the flat surface presents any holes, there are almost certain to be maggots in the umbrella part. The second fable was that mushrooms grow to their full size in a single night. The explanation for this might be that Wallace's Ground was so well known that no mushroom was ever allowed to grow for more than one day.

Mother's working journeys to the Field were in pursuit of less popular foods than mushrooms. She was a great wine maker, partly because she enjoyed any unusual form of catering, and partly in the hope that Father would spend less good money in bars. I do not think she ever took a drink herself, except for the sipping which is part of making good wine, when none of the ingredients were weighed or measured. In all her famous cookery I do not think Mother ever weighed or timed anything. Her only failures were in boiling eggs to get them to the exact state of liquidity which Father liked. She always took one up first and cut the top off to make sure how the others were getting along.

From the garden she made redcurrant, blackcurrant, potato and parsnip wines. From Wallace's Ground she collected dandelions, elderflowers and elderberries, plus wheat from the adjoining field. I repeat that I do not think she ever took a glassful, but she did come home one day with her hat very much on one side, and a very red face. This was not 'the drink', but she had been getting blackberries out of the hedge of Wallace's Ground in the very hot sun. It is the only time I remember seeing my Mother sunburnt; her generation never went out without a hat, and would use a parasol for any normal short walk.

In her old age, when my eldest brother was tenant of the farm, he often took Mother in his car on his evening tour of inspection. He knew that most of the land and the farming was unfamiliar to her, but he appreciated her love for Wallace's Ground. He must often have gone a good deal out of his way, and thought up a number of excuses for stopping in the Field, or by the middle gate. In some ways he was a very considerate man, and I think too that the Field meant a great deal to him. He certainly hated the interlude in its history when part of it was taken as a parish playing field.

My Father had no apparent special affection for the Ground. He died aged 90, and until his 87th year he could still manage to walk the hill from the village. I do not think he ever went on the farm without his gun, and was a reasonably good shot, without spectacles, nearly till the end of his life. There was always just the chance of a rabbit, through the first gate at the top of the hill. Once when I was with him he got a French partridge which flew up *from the bush* adjoining the gate. It was the first time I had ever seen a partridge except on the soil, or in the air. French partridges will perch, which makes sense of the old Christmas song about 'a partridge in a pear tree'. Till I had seen this shot of Father's I had despised the folk song, because no partridge in my life had been in a tree.

We held the shooting rights of Wallace's Ground and of the rest of the farm, since our landlords, Winchester College, were unlike a personal squire. The rights had always been sold by us for a few pounds to a 'gentleman-farmer' neighbour. Actually they were worth very little, and selling the rights does not include rabbits. None-the-less they certainly did include that French partridge. In many respects my Father was a puritan, and especially as far as honesty about money was concerned. Yet he was typical of most countrymen in failing to have any shame over poaching for the pot.

My two brothers were 12 and 15 years older than I was, and they were in partnership with my Father when I was a schoolboy. Both worked extremely hard alongside the men, setting the pace. Father spent most of his time dealing in fat cattle at the markets of Exeter, Sturminster Newton, Dorchester and Wimborne. I do not think I ever saw him doing any farm labour, although he helped on busy occasions in the butcher's job, say at Christmas time. If he turned up in Wallace's Ground on a haymaking evening, he might spend an hour leading horses with empty wagons from the stack to the men in the field, and bringing back the full loads. This was normally a job for a boy, but it could lead to wasted time, if two field gangs were both in action. Either one lot were without an empty wagon, or the rick gang were idle. It could not be done with less than five wagons, and was a worthwhile job for the boss to organise. Father did not do it for long. Shepherd had joined the haymaking gang in the afternoon and Father would tell him to stay with them. For himself he would take the ritual last look at the sheep. He then picked up his gun and left us. Just before dark we probably heard at least one gun shot in the distance. Two shots in sharp succession probably meant he had missed with both barrels.

Leaning on the gate of Wallace's Ground and looking back I think I am much nearer my Father in temperament than either of my brothers. They differed wildly from each other, but both could tolerate long hours of toil. Dad and I preferred living on our wits. He in dealing, and I in free-lance radio. We both made a fair bit of money, and had a lot of fun, but unfortunately neither of us managed to hold much of the money.

Of the men who taught me farming skills in Wallace's Ground my best memory is of Frank Lovelace, perhaps because he was only about five years my senior. This is not a big difference, but it was an enormous gulf in 1919, because I had just left school and Frank had served right through the war in France. It was typical of the man that he volunteered for an Army unit which uses horses. He had started work with us on leaving school, working the two odd horses which went with the farming system. A carter was in charge of three horses which pulled a double furrow plough on the light soil of Wallace's Ground. Three horses in a team were also used in most other farm jobs such as binding corn, or pulling large wagons. At our peak I think we had four teams of three, with two odd horses for lighter jobs. It was these two which Frank worked in his teens before the war.

When he came back from France it was to take on a full team. In fact he looked after four in his thatched stable, although he worked the usual team of three. I helped him in grooming and feeding in the evening, and sometimes worked the odd horse on light jobs.

Frank taught me how to lay out the first ridge across a field, which settles the straightness of the rest of the ploughing. I learnt how to set a plough for equal depth of furrow, and for better penetration in hard ground. He taught me how to turn corners with a binder, which is not as simple as it sounds, and to drill seed without wild wobbles being apparent where drill widths overlap.

I enjoyed the work of caring for horses, at least to some extent, although I wanted a tractor. I never should have made a good ploughman in those old horse days. I did not like walking 10 miles per day in a flinty furrow, and the concentration required was of the wrong sort for me. It did not occupy my whole mind and imagination – or at least that is the way I like to describe it. The fact is that my attention was for ever wandering.

Frank must have come home from France, on leave, during our harvest period when I was on holiday from school. I remember the occasion because we were building an oat stack just across the lane from Wallace's Ground, and were sitting in the shade for our midday meal. Most of the conversation naturally centred on war, and on life in the countryside and towns in France. For the first time in my life I was shown photographs of naked girls. One or two of the older men refused to look at such filthy pictures. Others were quite obviously pleasantly stimulated by photos which they had heard existed, but had never seen. I was the only youngster present, and I think all the others were married, and familiar with the sight of the bare female form. It is no virtue on my part, but it is a fact that my main feeling was disappointment. These pictures left nothing to the imagination, and nakedness was less alluring than a little clothing.

Frank continued to work on the farm for the whole of his life, and always with horses. I think my brother kept one team for several years after the tractors were fully established, mainly because Frank would have left if he had been asked to work without them. In fact at one time, when my eldest brother held the shop and the farm it was decided that a foreman was necessary. Frank was sounded tactfully, but the offer of extra money did not tempt him from his horses. Looking back I do not think he would have enjoyed giving orders to his old friends. I am also fairly sure that my brother was most wise to keep that last horse team. Even today there is a perfectly good case to be made for one working horse on a farm. For odd jobs and relatively light loads most tractors are working far below capacity, and are expensive. The trouble would be finding a man to use a horse. Plenty of girls would undertake it, but the haulage tasks I have in mind often involve the driver in some fairly heavy lifting.

Frank's old father, Bill, first taught me how to build a haystack in Wallace's Ground, long before the days of hay balers. In the adjoining field he also taught me how the same principles applied to ricks of sheaves. Bill was a very remarkable man. I do not know if he was born lame, but for all the years I knew him he had a leg which was bent at the knee and permanently stiff. This kept him out of the better paid farm jobs involving the care of livestock, yet it was amazing what he could do.

For anyone who has ever seen a stack built it is fantastic that a very lame man should do the placing of the sheaves on the very edge of the walls, or manage the tall tapering of the roof. Yet old Bill did it, and even entered his stacks in the competitions run by the Dorchester Agricultural Society. In addition he could keep up with the fittest men in singling swedes and mangolds. Presumably the hoe took the supporting place of his stick, and the distances walked were not great. This work of hoeing to leave the plants single in rows was paid at so much per acre and old Bill could earn good money.

The first shepherd I remember in Wallace's Ground was named Jeanes. The shepherds of those days were the most important and responsible men on the farm. A curious result of the respect with which I regarded shepherd is that I cannot now recall his Christian name. The other employees were Frank, Bill, Charlie, Fred and so on, but 'Shep' was used invariably in talking to him, or about him. It was a badge of rank rather like 'Sergeant' in the Army.

He was a tall very strong man, and reasonably prosperous since his wage was relatively high, and his wife was the unofficial village mid-wife, and 'layer-out' of the dead. This work of hers, at the very beginning and the very end of life, sounds curious but was common in many villages. I think she had received some real training and was always known as Nurse Jeanes.

Shep taught me some of the elements of shepherding in Wallace's Ground, but my chief memory of him was in a neighbouring field and had nothing to do with sheep. My Father was not a ram breeder and our flock had no elaborate trimming of the fleece to be done in preparation for autumn shows and fairs. In addition the fact that Dorset Horn sheep lamb in October, meant that August was a relatively slack time for shepherd. He could and did volunteer to help in the harvest field, and received a lump sum of 'harvest money'. All regular workers received this lump sum and there was no overtime rates. It meant that the harder they worked the sooner harvest would be over, and the quicker they got the sum, which usually went on winter clothing. Bad weather at harvest was almost as big a curse to them as to the farmer. No doubt a lot of folk-lore about picking up the last sheaf had its roots in this bad old system of a lump sum for harvest overtime. I say bad because men who were desperately short of money had to share the farmer's risk of a long expensive harvest. The farmers were not getting a fat living, but the workers should not have been forced to work for less in wet weather.

My present point, however, is that Shep Jeanes was a volunteer for harvest work, and welcome because of his strength. His influence on me was to partner me in a day's work which tested me to the full. I was about 15 at the time, and reasonably good at painful sporting events such as cross-country running. Harvest work with Shep taught me for the first time that I was man enough to keep up with any worker on the farm.

Corn was cut with horse drawn binders, and the sheaves

were 'stooked' in groups of 8 or 10. It was usual for two men to work together taking five lines of sheaves at a time. At the beginning of the day we had to wait until the first five lines had been cut, because they were carried to be stooked on the fifth line. This meant that they were as far from the hedge as possible, and would get the best of the drying wind and sun. Thereafter we made our lines of stooks on the middle line of each five. You went round the field with the butts of the sheaves towards you and picked them up by the middle to tuck one under each arm. Then you and your partner faced each other, and let the sheaves slide down your legs. At the same time you drew the ears together, so that you had started a stook with four sheaves standing upright; each pair inclining slightly to the next. When five pairs were in position they would shoot off the rain, and stand any reasonable amount of wind.

Obviously when two men were taking five lines the least walking was involved by each taking all the sheaves in two lines, and alternatively picking up the sheaves from the middle line which marked the place for the stooks. When a boy was working with a man it was quite usual for the man to collect from three lines while the boy dealt with only two. On this occasion Shep insisted on my taking my share of the fifth line. What was more we kept up with the binder all day and finished by catching the last sheaf it threw out. The normal working day was reckoned at 10–12 acres for each pair of stookers, depending on the thickness of the crop. In a good piece of wheat we had done 15 acres, and I had qualified as a man. We were a mile from home and I was utterly weary. It was a relief when Carter Ike Collins let me ride one of his great shire horses home.

Old Ike had the care of four horses, and their summer grazing was in the field adjoining Wallace's Ground called Putt Ground – heaven knows why. A putt with us was a two wheeled cart usually associated with hauling dung. Ike was a quiet, patient, old man, very gentle with horses. He was more than a little deaf and had only one pace for himself or his horses. No emergency would make him hurry and I only once saw his placid nature disturbed. His wife Louisa was his opposite in being fond of cheerful conversation, and she was a fast, loud speaker. She had a distinct weakness for a pint of beer, and spent many evenings in the pub, which in those days was not respectable for women. During the 1914 War she became a post woman, and had quite a bit of money to spend. One Saturday Ike went to the pub to fetch her, and they came back for 100 yards down the village street, in unusual fashion. Loo trotted unsteadily ahead saying 'don't 'e Ike', and Ike followed silently, making wild swings at her with his leather belt. He missed each time until she slipped and fell. For the first time the village realised that under voluminous skirts and petticoats Loo wore no bloomers.

She had her place in Wallace's Ground because she was never busy in her house, but always ready to pick blackberries and crabapples for the price of a drink. I have also known her to take Ike's horses to the Field for grazing, to save the old man the walk up the hill. She was a cheerful, good-hearted soul, apart from her one weakness.

The memory of a second day's stooking, and the ride home on Ike's biggest horse, is a reminder that the word 'stook' is completely alien to Wallace's Ground. I have used it because it is understood by most districts of Britain. The Dorset word was 'hile' although that may not be a correct spelling; I have never seen it written. Possibly it derives from 'aisle'; the long rows of stooked sheaves had a faint resemblance to the pillars of a church.

Other men who have impressed me for many years in Wallace's Ground were quite different from old Ike and Frank Lovelace. Both of these were devoted to horses, and had little interest in machines. Frank was perfectly capable of maintaining the tools in his charge such as mowing machines and selfbinders, but Ike was quite dumb mechanically. At the opposite extreme there were a number of men, well into middle-age, who took to tractors in a remarkable manner. Joe Barrett had grown up children when he first met an internal combustion engine, but he delighted in all things mechanical. His school education had probably ceased about twelve, and the only training he had received was as a keeper. Yet Joe could diagnose trouble, and do anything with the aid of very primitive tools.

This ability to deal with machines is heartening when we look away from this 'Field in Dorset', out to the distant parts of the earth. New words have been coined such as 'under-privileged' and 'developing' to describe uneducated people, living on insufficient food. It is desirable to remember that 40 years ago there were many illiterate countrymen, existing on little more than a starvation diet. These men worked the combine harvesters in the 1939 War.

I seem to remember a hymn which claims 'O'er heathen lands afar, thick darkness broodeth yet.' It was certainly dark for the Agricultural Worker in the 1930s. There is plenty of evidence that middle class children were taller and heavier at the same stage in their schooling, yet the under-privileged were completely capable of learning new productive techniques in our land. There is real advancement, as a near certainty, if aid is given to needy nations in new tools, seeds and fertilisers. Backward human communities are capable of learning new techniques in a very short time, and experience in Wallace's Ground with Englishmen persuades me that it is little to do with academic education.

Understanding of machines has not much connection with literacy, and the most backward races will contain a sufficiency of born mechanics. My personal performance supports this. I have no liking for servicing tractors, and at the best was always a slow worker with my hands. My education included graduating in agricultural science from a University, and I have a theory that most educated men could force themselves to do most jobs adequately. The tone-deaf may not be able to learn to sing nor the colour blind to paint. Apart from this, by a great effort all of us could cook, or paper the parlour, or discover how to adjust a combine harvester. A few of us – irrespective of race or training – are wizards with machines, without having acquired the least skill in writing or reading. There is evidence that Pakistan may soon have surplus cereals for the world markets, whereas a few years ago it had a peasantry in danger of famine.

Wallace's Ground has known many men who have gone

through an agricultural revolution without any difficulty in learning a new way of life. I have a feeling of inferiority in their presence, which is very different from pride in being able to keep up with Shep Jeanes in stooking, or standing in for Bill Lovelace in building a stack.

On the whole the born mechanics in the Field have not necessarily been men who were highly skilled in the old hand arts of farming. Layering a hedge, shearing a sheep, splitting hazel rods to make hurdles, or drawing a straight furrow, made the leading workers of the past. What they had in common with the key men of the present was a strong left wing tradition in politics. There is no doubt that very able farm workers have always had a feeling that they were grossly underpaid.

In the past this Socialism in politics was almost always combined with non-conformity in religion. This is much less common today, and of course it did not apply in every case. Frank Lovelace probably voted Labour, but he was not an outstanding pillar of the Chapel nor of the Workers Union. George Bollen on the other hand walked miles every Sunday as a Local Preacher. He was the strongest man who ever worked in the Field in my time, and was fiercely individualistic. He took a regular wage at harvest time, but spent the rest of the year as a piece worker at hedging, hoeing and shearing.

Another outstanding man who worked with me in the Field was Fred Perris. He was a keen non-conformist, but I do not think he preached. This was in an age when a known Union man stood in some peril of being victimised. My Father had no strong feelings about what were usually known as 'agitators', but some farmers certainly did. Fred made no secret of his membership of a Worker's Union, but he was one of the quickest, and most intelligent workers on the farm. From the days of the Tolpuddle Martyrs there has been a tradition of the best men being politically Left. George Loveless was spokesman for the Martyrs; he was a local preacher, and his worst enemies never questioned the fact that he was an able and conscientious worker. In the case of our Fred Perris, his combination of hard work and puritan living resulted in his being able to achieve independence. He became a market gardener in the village. From memory I do not think he employed much labour outside his family but I have often wondered what sort of employer he would be for whom to work.

Two of the biggest farmers in the district had started in life as farm workers, and had been staunch followers of Joseph Arch. The name Arch was still remembered in my boyhood as a leader of agricultural workers, but he had come to be regarded as a moderate. In a way the whole thing was similar to my maiden aunt's feeling about Liberalism. She was a Tory, but felt that 'dear Mr Gladstone' was quite different from Radicals like Asquith.

Our farming neighbours had no regrets about their youthful following of Arch, he was quite different from modern Socialist agitators. As employers they must have been satisfactory, because their men stayed with them. I don't think that their early struggles made them extra generous with pay, and they certainly knew if a man was giving a fair day's work. Probably Fred Perris acted similarly with any paid labour, and it is a basis of respect. The men who worked for the squire in a nearby village, received standard wages, but got away with a less strenuous life. Their boss knew nothing about doing the job himself.

This applied to the old type squires, who did not expect their home farm to pay, nor hoped for any high income from rented land. Their money came from industrial interests, and the estate gave them sport and a social position. Looking across the fields from Wallace's Ground I wonder how the labour-boss relationship will work in future. For a century the Field has been farmed by my family, who were working farmers, and could set the pace for employees. My nephew carries on the tradition, but he is probably the last Wightman to hold the tenancy.

After him Wallace's is likely to be farmed by a company who own most of the land in the village. They are new squires only similar to the old in not doing physical work with their men. Under them the farm must pay, and their lack of knowledge of skilled jobs no longer matters. The old hand arts have been replaced by machines, and the new squires would soon be after their local farm manager if the machines were not working at their known capacity.

Actually the working of machines to their known capacity is not quite as simple to enforce as it sounds. The men of Wallace's Ground still have a considerable power in fixing what work is done in a day, without apparently wasting time. In fact they are not wasting time any more than Frank Lovelace was doing when he kept his horses at a slow plodding speed. They could not keep up all day the pace they were quite prepared to take in early morning. Machines obviously do not suffer in quite the same way, but the driver certainly can. The tractor has brought two new factors which affect the drivers – noise and jolting. Generally speaking the higher the speed and power the more these become serious.

Many town friends in the early days of tractors asked why the driver so often spent much of his driving time standing up. One look at the primitive metal seats was enough to explain this, but modern well sprung and padded seats do not entirely cure the trouble. Jolting is bound to occur and it becomes progressively worse as speed increases. In addition the law requires safety cabs to be fitted to new tractors, and these may make it impossible for the driver to escape jolting by standing, apart from increasing noise.

The law requiring safety cabs to be fitted to new tractors after September, 1970 was badly drafted, and the manufacturers were curiously unco-operative in some cases. They sometimes offered a standard cab which gave the customer no choice. The law allowed a cab to be merely a strong frame, which provided safety against overturning, but afforded no shelter against wind and rain. This sounds undesirable but it was not until the late 1960s that farmers had started to be conscious of the deafness which could arise from the drumming noise in a cab.

When some shelter was felt to be desirable there was little doubt that noise could be reduced if the sides and roof of the cab were of plastic materials. Yet in a few cases there was no choice from metal cladding, which was noisier and more expensive.

Manufacturers admit that tractors will have to be redesigned to reduce noise, and in the meantime they provide free ear muffs. To obtain anything approaching the lack of noise which we expect in a car the tractor cab would need to have joints between panels and frame separated by some sort of rubbery material. In addition a floor would be an absolute essential. Such cabs exist in America and would add £500 to the cost of a tractor here.

The combined result of jolting and noise is to force a driver to reduce speed. He may do this almost unconsciously, late in the day when he is nerve-weary. The boss or foreman will find it extremely difficult to spot that the machine is working below capacity. Speed is not easy to estimate with a tractor moving at a distance, and the driver can claim that the soil prevents faster travel, or that the engine needs tuning. The men of the Ground have always set the pace of work, and they always will. Output depends on goodwill, and on the farmer removing all irritations within his power.

To me there is a real danger that the future farmers of Wallace's Ground will be unable to understand fully the feelings of the men who work their machines, or care for their livestock. They may pay higher wages, improve farm buildings to enable quicker work, and generally be ideal employers. There always has been a fellowship between the working farmer and his staff which is hard to define, and it is not much to do with any ordinary specification of what makes a good boss. Working with a man is about the only way to understand him. Once it was easy to acquire such understanding because so many jobs were shared. Today a man can be alone and do the entire work of the old harvesting and threshing gangs with one expensive machine. How is it possible for the farmer to enjoy fellowship with such a man?

The answer is to relieve him for a weekly day off, and to learn the truth of constant concentration on all the machine is doing, plus the jolting, the dust and the loneliness. The working farmer can do it; the city executive may not realise its importance.

Every part of my life has been influenced by the men I have known in Wallace's Ground. It seems a far cry from this Field in Dorset to broadcasting, yet it was the Field which gave truth and sincerity to anything I ever said. It is impossible to cheat with the soil for very long, and a microphone picks out insincerity of words in a strangely cruel way.

The men of the Ground formed me for good or ill, and I am certain that they had been made in their turn by this 'blessed plot of earth'. There is a difference between the men of the high mountains, and those from flat, fertile fen. Within six miles of Wallace's Ground there is wet clay which is practically unploughable, and where for seven months of the year cows must not be allowed to tread on the sodden soil. The men of those fields are a different breed, with different virtues and faults.

I have no ambition for the magnificence of the high hills, nor for the amazing fertility of the market garden fields of Lincoln. The wet clay pastures with their host of cows are not to my taste. I am content with this dry, rolling upland, on thin chalk soil. As Mother always said 'the air is different in Wallace's Ground'.

Chapter Seven

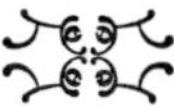

Land Everlasting

It is difficult to describe how Wallace's Ground can meet the human longing for an abiding place, when obviously it has changed so much in my memory. 'Change and decay' do not always go together; anything living will change. Probably all I am asking is that this land will continue to be farmed, and that seems extremely likely to happen.

The word 'conservancy' can be very misleading if it seems to mean a complete lack of change, and to many people this is precisely what it does imply. There is a danger that country lovers will concentrate far too much on what farmers are doing in the way of hedge trimming, tree felling and the use of chemicals on the land. A great deal more harm can be done from outside, by those who seek amenities in fine weather. They want the countryside to remain as it was, or rather as they sentimentally remember it. This applies to almost all of us in some degree, especially when the land is held by others.

I like the well trimmed hedges of Wallace's Ground, yet dislike seeing a well drained pasture, half a mile away, on what was derelict withy bed in my childhood. Withy is a dialect word for a species of willow, and I have no logical desire to see this bush conserved, nor the other swamp plants that went with it. My regret is connected with the memory of childhood games in the thickets, that future generations will be unable to enjoy. It is the more unreasonable on my part because I realise that even village children no longer have much freedom of access to privately owned land.

In my childhood we knew that we must keep out of crops, but we could play ball games in any pasture with no one objecting. The coppices and woodlands were officially banned when pheasants were breeding, but dodging a keeper was part of the fun. In any case there were very few of us, and the fact that we had to avoid being seen or heard probably meant that we did little to alarm the birds.

In all the modern concern that cities should be able to enjoy countryside amenities it is seldom realised that country children lost the enjoyment of amenities at least a couple of generations ago. The history of Wallace's Ground illustrates what I mean. I forget the precise date when the Parish Council acquired part of it as a playing field but it was before 1950. Previously children had often played football there, but there was no village football team, and village cricket had a shaky existence which went back to about 1922. If adults played football it was normally only on Good Friday because farm workers had a six day week until about 1938, even when they were not concerned with livestock. Older men could play cricket, such as the vicar, which accounts for a cricket eleven being just possible. Neither for Good Friday football nor for summer cricket was there any question raised about paying rent for the use of the land.

Undoubtedly the half day weekly holiday for workers was a major reason why the Parish decided to take over part of Wallace's Ground, but it was not the sole reason. Grassland was being used much more intensively and a weekly football match damaged the turf for grazing. On the other hand the team never knew when the farmer would decide to plough the land, and they would lose their pitch. The ploughing question might appear to have always been a hazard in the days when playing was a free amenity, but it was most unlikely to happen.

It was well after the 1914–18 War that it was realised how easily a new pasture could be established. Sir George Stapledon was being revolutionary when he preached that the quickest way to improve a poor pasture was to plough it and reseed. Through all my youth a tenant farmer faced a large penalty if he ploughed permanent pasture. I mentioned this in Chapter One. It meant that if the villagers were allowed to play games in a grass field they were reasonably certain it would not be ploughed. The main trouble was the increasing reluctance of the farmer to allow regular adult games. This extended to forbidding free access to children, especially in the summer holidays when town visitors were common.

Wallace's Ground was given up as a playing field by the Parish for a number of reasons. It had a pronounced slope, and the climb from the village was unpopular. For several years the parish had no amenity. The children could play cowboys and Indians in several leafy lanes, but the roads were utterly impossible for ball games, and they were much worse off for amenities than we had ever been. In 1969–70 the Council acquired a new playing field in the valley, on about the only flat land in the parish.

In passing, this land would never have been considered in the days when we lost part of Wallace's Ground, and it would make any old Councillor turn in his grave. It illustrates how farming and land use now changes in a very short time. The new sports field is part of what was a water-meadow, which means that it used to be worth four times as much as any other pasture in the village. It was laid out in ridges and furrows which let water flow over the land in winter. This raised the soil temperature, and grass just outside the flow of water was a good month later in starting growth in spring.

Today the labour of clearing ditches and regulating water flow is too high. The surface of part of the meadow has had its ridges and ditches bulldozed to give a truly level playing field. My nephew on the Parish Council has been concerned with making this village amenity, and I do not think the farmer of the water-meadow feels very strongly about it. I look down from Wallace's Ground and remember how much my brother disliked the earlier partition of the Field. It is ironic that the Council Chairman who arranged the first playing field was the occupier of the water-meadow. Now part of his most valuable land has gone and we have regained the lost acres of Wallace's Ground.

That sort of thing will certainly happen again, but there seems no immediate danger that the Field will cease to be farmed. One field just across the lane illustrates the sort of change which does not alarm me. In my Father's youth it was an ordinary stretch of arable. By my boyhood it had been turned into allotments for the deserving poor, who used it solely for growing potatoes. We allowed our own men the use of horses and a plough on a Saturday afternoon in spring if they had an allotment.

These allotments were long narrow strips, exactly like those encouraged in towns during the wars, for increasing national food production. The country village allotments formed at the turn of the century were nothing to do with the national food supply, but were regarded as a charity. They were provided by the landowner, and tenant farmers were annoyed if the field happened to be part of their acreage. In some ways the allotments were fairly typical of Victorian charity. The total rent of the strips was more than the original rent of the whole field, so that the landlord lost absolutely nothing. The only result was that a strong sober worker, after long hours of poorly paid toil, could grow some food for his family.

The use of the allotments solely for potatoes was later copied in the towns. The point was that the fields were remote from dwellings. Other vegetables can be stolen quickly, but potatoes have to be dug up, which is a fairly slow job. In addition our forefathers believed that potatoes could be grown safely without any rotation of crops. It was after 1930 before I first became familiar with the sight of crop failures due to too frequent cropping, and I was an agricultural scientist. Town and country allotment holders knew nothing of the tiny soil eelworm which stunted their crops.

What happened was that an allotment holder gave up his plot because his potatoes were so small. For a time there was always another man ready to take the allotment because he was convinced that his predecessor had been a poor cultivator, or had used indifferent seed, or insufficient fertiliser. It took quite a few years before it was accepted that the land was potato sick.

The Allotment Field across the lane from Wallace's Ground followed the usual eelworm pattern of having scattered plots unoccupied, followed by more abandoned than cultivated land. The next step was for a market gardener to take the whole field for vegetable crops other than potatoes. Presumably he paid less per acre than the plot rent, but more than was paid on a sizeable farm. Finally he found that growing vegetables in the open is not very profitable at a distance from any centre of population, and on soil with no high natural fertility. Once more the allotments became part of our neighbour's farm, after a chequered history of sixty years.

Change does not destroy the feeling that a field is an abiding place, as long as the soil remains exposed to the wind, the rain and the sun, or any concrete patch is a small portion aimed at keeping more animals. Only when concrete sweeps over most of the surface is the earth destroyed. I think Wallace's Ground would still be abiding for me if it was planted with trees, which is going a very long way from anything it has yet experienced.

There are two fields in the valley which can be seen from the Ground, which used to be planted with apple trees, but have now been cleared. One is still used as a small grazing paddock, whereas once it was not only a paddock but a source of cider apples. I can look down on it and remember the exact position of three trees which were reasonably good for cooking or eating raw. Old-fashioned cider fruit was too sweet, or too sour, or had a curious dry bitter-sweet taste. All the boys in the village knew the tasty trees, and no one minded theft for personal consumption.

The other little orchard has been destroyed completely by a village housing scheme. It has wiped out the house where I was born, Frank Lovelace's four-horse stable, some piggeries, an old barn, a huge dung heap, and the old uneconomic apple trees. It is a well laid out housing estate, with well-kept gardens, but for me a bit of my sort of country has been destroyed, never to return. It is ironic to find it signposted as 'Wightman's Orchard'.

Wallace's Ground has always been important in my personal feelings, but as an abiding place it has changed with increasing age. A few people may have felt the same emotional change with a house, especially if it happens to be an old house. I have lived as a tenant in the same house for over forty years, and the date over the window is 1573. Probably this date was carved in Victorian times, but the walls and fire places make it fairly certain that it was built in Tudor times. The first owner was probably a fairly prosperous tradesman, possibly in the linen trade. The place is too big to be the cottage of a farm worker, but could have been a farm house, as it was in 1914.

Whoever built it used some second-hand stone, probably from a religious house abolished in the Reformation. There are carved pillars which were never transported for twenty miles to form part of a small house. The old oak beams could have been local, because a strip of clay soil, suitable for trees, is only a mile away.

When I first came here in my youth I liked it because the rooms were fairly big, and the walls fairly soundproof. Today I look through the iron bars on the mullioned windows, and think of how many people have lived, and loved, and sorrowed here. I also wonder how many more men and women will come after me. They may alter the rooms, or stairs, or install central heating, but it could have another four centuries as a dwelling place.

Something very similar has developed in my feeling for Wallace's Ground. It was just a pleasant field, a shade more desirable than other fields on the farm, and overlooking the sheltered village. Men had altered it in past centuries, and will alter it again in the centuries to come. With old age in sight I have become more and more conscious of the fleeting nature of human life. It has become a labour to walk up the hill to the Field just as it did for my Father and Mother. I am not an important part of life, and certainly not the centre of it all. Only the enduring field can stand for Life Everlasting, and, strangely, there is no unhappiness in such a thought, or in the fact that the field could go.

I remember a talk by Arthur Street in a series called 'Dear to my Heart', which was broadcast from Bristol in 1956. He described how he always stopped at the brow of the hill on his way home from his chalkland farm. It is a farm with less hedges than my chalk land, but the shape of the rounded upland and the sudden valley are similar. Arthur's pleasure in tidy, mechanised cropping was very like my own about Wallace's Ground, yet in one respect we differ. The hills of home brought him many happy memories of country sports.

This was never true in my case. I enjoyed ferreting the hedge banks of Wallace's Ground, but this was vermin control, and not dignified by the name of sport. In my youth I had no moral objection to any form of hunting. Children are not horrified by killing, especially country children. There was even a fascination in visiting the local slaughterhouse and seeing a pig having its throat cut – humane stunning devices were unknown in those days. Killing for fun was completely natural, and the only reason I did not go fox hunting was because my family was not rich enough to keep pleasure horses.

Only relatively rich farming families could provide ponies for the young, except when poorer men had a notable skill in breeding and training hunters, so that they could make their hunting pay. This did not apply to any of my family, and in any case my generation were much more interested in motorbikes. Following fox hounds on foot was likely to lead to many days when the fox ran straight, and you saw nothing of the hunt after he had been driven from cover.

Beagles hunting the hare could be kept in sight, and in fact mounted followers were banned. The hare usually runs in a wide circle, and the very elderly can stand on a bit of high ground and see a lot of the hunt. Otter hounds, when they have found an otter, are moving at the rate at which the otter swims, so that they can be followed at a walk. Badgers are dug out from their deep labyrinth of burrows, so that spectators usually do nothing but stand still.

I have seen a badger dig in Wallace's Ground, and fox hounds have dashed across the Field behind a fox, which was found in Kingcombe and made for King Grove. The names are a reminder that my village once had a royal owner, the Norman wife of the Saxon King Ethelred. Still the Kings of those days hunted the deer, and we were well outside any royal hunting centre.

Apart from my Father's shooting, the only other blood sport I have seen in Wallace's Ground was quite unofficial. In College vacations I did quite a lot of shepherding, and had a mongrel dog. He looked like a very large black and white collie, apart from possessing no tail. Bob could run down a hare, and I fear I made no effort to stop him. This is very bad behaviour in a sheep dog, because it might have made him rough with sheep, but I enjoyed eating hare. It was also very thrilling to have a one dog private coursing match. I liked it as much as Bob, and it seemed not to have any serious effect on his handling of sheep.

In mature middle age I turned against field sport, but I do not swear that if I owned another Bob I should restrain him if he put up a hare in Wallace's Ground. Apart from this confession, my approach to hunting is reasonably logical. There are some wild animals which can be pests in agriculture or forestry if they become too numerous. This applies to foxes, rabbits, the deer and the hare. Only occasionally is a badger or an otter any menace to livestock, timber or farm crops.

I would therefore rule out badger digging and otter hunting. Badgers will take poultry, and otters do some damage to salmon, but much more by rolling in watercress beds. If they must be stopped locally, there are painless ways of doing it. Digging and hunting are cruel, and designed to give a thrill to the lower instincts in man, similar to bull baiting and cock fighting.

Rabbit killing was never called a sport, although there is a thrill in ferreting when the weather is reasonable, and the rabbits bolt from their burrows fairly quickly. Nothing is much more boring than the rabbit which stays underground, and is killed there by the ferret, who then is said to 'lie up'. I do not regard ferreting as a cruel way of killing rabbits. Killing the hare is connected with two forms of sport. They can be hunted by a pack of beagles who follow their scent, and slowly tire them to complete exhaustion. This is hard to justify because beagles are at their best when hares are scarce, and there is little agricultural reason for reducing them. Where the hare is a pest the beagles are apt to put up far too many, and to split the pack, or to change from an exhausted to a fresh hare. Coursing by greyhounds needs a fair number of hares. The hounds hunt by sight, and are very fast so there is no prolonged agony. On the whole, however, I favour shooting. The hare is an easy target, and with a good dog a wounded hair is unlikely to escape.

Fox hunting is probably still the most humane way of keeping foxes under control, but some of the claims made for it take a lot of believing. For instance, it is said that a fox feels no fear until he has almost reached the point of exhaustion and death. In support it has been said that a hunted fox has killed a couple of hens in a farm yard with the hounds in full cry. It seems to me that snapping at a hen by a fox is no sign that he is free from fear. It is certainly true that a hunted fox will sometimes lie down and relax if hounds check, and there is a break in hound music. This is a perfectly natural reaction. He thinks he has escaped and animals have little of the human imagination and memory of danger. The fox has few natural enemies, but a hare will relax in exactly the same way, and it is in peril a dozen times a day from wild predators.

As to the deer, they can undoubtedly be controlled by shooting and this can also lead to a healthier stock. In hunting a great deal of trouble is taken to select a good stag, but controlling shooting can get rid of indifferent animals. I am not thinking of any carefree shooting with a shot gun, which is almost certain to lead to wounding and a slow death. A rifle is necessary, which means a single bullet and a rifle has a long range. Supporters of hunting have said that deer could not be shot in a relatively thickly populated district, such as Dorset, because of the distance a bullet might travel. A shot gun has a range of about fifty yards, but a rifle bullet could kill at much more than ten times this distance. Spreading small shot from a 12 bore gun is used for a moving hare or a flying bird. Seldom could a man with a rifle be sure that he would hit a vital spot, even in a stationary deer with no risk that his one bullet would not miss and endanger other lives. The only way to make sure is to put the man with the rifle up a tree. There he is shooting towards the earth. Grazing deer seldom look up, and in any case he can make a 'hide' in advance from branches. He has plenty of time to aim and can select any deer which is weakly, or past its best. Planned shooting by trained men on these lines can fix a figure in advance for the number which should be culled.

From these remarks on country sports it will be obvious that nothing in the view from Wallace's Ground brings me much in the way of memories of killing for fun. My tastes happen to have been for ball games rather than field sports. But even when Wallace's Ground was the village Sports Field it did not bring me many joys. The conditions were never very good, and I had got used to college pitches. Village bowlers are at least as fast as those playing for good clubs, and I have known a first class county bat to be thankful when he was out for a duck in Wallace's Ground.

I am fully conscious that it is a sign of conceited snobbery to claim that I was too good a player to enjoy games on village pitches. The truth is that I was dead scared of fast bowling which was almost out of reach on the off, but bounced just clear of the back of my head. One thing about field sports is a strange absence of snobbery, which outsiders may not believe. The Master is always treated with great respect, but so is the skipper of a cricket team. I have never been snubbed as an inferior, even when following hounds on foot. This was long before I possessed any fame as a radio broadcaster. It is one good side of hunting which I do not remember having seen mentioned before. Not that it makes any difference to my opinion that blood sports should have died with cock fighting, and the knowledge that cock fighting still takes place in secret strengthens my view. Men have cruel instincts.

There is nothing that can be written to change the men who talk of field sports and those who use the term blood sports. Neither side have much to do with my feeling for Wallace's Ground as an abiding place, or what has come to me to be a sanctuary. This is a word I hesitate to use, because for most people sanctuary has a deep religious significance. I am using it in a homelier manner, and in a sense which it is easier to feel in the country than in towns.

The Field has changed, but the changes are welcome. Dorset has a great poet who wrote in the last century, but he is little known outside Dorset because he wrote in the Dorset dialect. I class William Barnes with Robert Burns who also wrote in dialect, but one appealed to a nation and the other to one small rural county. Barnes expressed much of my thoughts about the changes in Wallace's Ground in *Our Fathers' Works*. For instance, the lay-out of the hedges:

'Be works that we've a-found a-wrought
By our forefathers' care and thought'

I have altered his spelling from the old Dorset pronunciation because it is difficult to recognise ceare as care.

Barnes goes on:

'They cleared the ground for grass to take
The place that bore the bramble break'

The brambles had been cleared before my time, but two thousand years ago this little hill may well have been covered in brambles and small bushes. Forest trees seldom grow on a few inches of soil over grass. Old Barnes knew all about his countryside which is more than can be said for all poets.

I want to quote the last verse of *Our Fathers' Works* and,

reluctantly, I have changed the dialect spelling. To be reasonably truthful I can drop unconsciously into the dialect pronunciation of such words as 'zoo' for 'so', but I find it difficult to read.

'So now may none of us forget
The pattern our forefathers set;
But each be fain to undertake
Some work to make for others gain,
That we might leave more good to share,
Less ills to bear, less souls to grieve,
And when our hands do fall to rest,
It might be from a-work a-blest.'

My Grandfather, Father, eldest brother and his son were, and are all people with normal human faults. I think they have done, and are doing something to leave 'more good to share, less ills to bear, less souls to grieve'. To me the symbol of it all is Wallace's Ground.

My Grandfather knew Barnes, who had a school in Dorchester and later a vicarage two miles outside the town. Father said he had a 'serene and happy face', whereas Hardy, as I remember him, was shrunken, with his face marked in unhappy lines. What is left for an ageing agnostic? Barnes had a sure and certain hope, but the lines on his face were partly made by a lifetime of gentle Christian behaviour. As far as I know Hardy had lived a moral, temperate life, but there was no peace in his face. The modern muck raking which gives him an illegitimate son seems to be based on unreliable evidence. He has been accused by local people of being 'a mean old so-and-so' but for a man of his fame there must have been endless calls on his purse. I think the two men could well have been alike as far as morality is concerned, and differed only in their reaction to the Faith. My own face is marked by old excesses, but Wallace's Ground is 'a-work a-blest', and the Faith is kind to sinners.

I have actually had very little to do with the farming of the Field, apart from giving my brother scientific advice about fertilisers and sheep diseases. I wrote that the feeling of sanctuary is easier to feel in the country than in the town. This may not be quite true, but I think there is something in it. Old William Barnes expressed the intense feeling a man can have for his own land :

> 'I got two fields and I don't care
> What squire may have a bigger share'

I have never been even the tenant of Wallace's Ground, and none of my family are ever likely to own it. Yet I think my nephew feels something of the same need for an abiding place on these little Dorset hills. In 1969 he paid far too much money to buy some neighbouring land from which he can look down on the village and up to the wide sky. I assured him at the time that it was completely economic, and because land values are still rising, his buy was not wildly extravagant. Yet at age 45 he knows as well as I do that he wanted a safe place on the little Dorset hills as home.

The temptation to be sentimental is very great, and it gets stronger as the years pass. I have to remind myself that an insurance company would give me ten more years of life if I asked for an annuity. Yet ten years were infinitely more important in my teens, when the Field could have been little more to me than a factory. Most other fields on the farm were places of toil where food was produced, and where I became extremely tired. Also there is absolutely no connection between Wallace's Ground and romance: my courting was done in other fields.

I do not think my feeling for this place has any connection with the fact that it was my Mother's favourite spot on earth. Most of my boyhood admiration was for my Father, and he had no strong affection for the Field. I hasten to add that I was very fond of my Mother, who was kind and good. My admiration for Father was because he had an original mind. If there is any justification for my copious writings and broadcastings it could be blamed on Father. At a very young age I took pleasure in hearing from him ideas which were not then in the conventional pattern of life.

He was a Christian by profession and actions, but he certainly did not believe in the general view of the resurrection of the body. He thought he would have some future contact with my two dead sisters but he had no fragment of belief that he would see them again as young girls, or babies, or as kindly mature women. Perhaps that view of the resurrection has had something to do with my feeling for Wallace's Ground.

In a way I hope it has not. I have dead friends I hope to see again as they were, and not in some nebulous spirit form. I do not think that immortality simply means having children to succeed you. There is a very easy impression of the resurrection in Wallace's Ground every spring. Every autumn I hope I shall live to see another spring in the Field. But all it means is more miraculous beauty, a fresh start in growing human food, a gift from a very good God. It is not the Resurrection and the Life, but something much less. The spring glory is an underserved gift. Wallace's Ground in spring, summer, autumn and winter is just home for me. I know it must be used in farming if it is to be kept alive. In this Field I have seen the great silver moon and the red sun in the sky together, but every countryman is familiar with such a sight on a harvest evening. This is a very ordinary place. Only in the undesired, endless leisure of a human autumn is it possible to stare long enough to take in the marvel of the ordinary.

Home is a pleasant place, but with nothing to do with immortality. I hope the Field goes on to give quiet pleasure to other generations. It is not 'land everlasting', indeed the word everlasting used to frighten me. Remember a speech Shakespeare put into the mouth of Mark Antony – 'The evil that men do lives after them, the good is oft interred with their bones.'

Somehow Wallace's Ground has taught me that the reverse is true. Evils live on in the Field in the shape of weeds, animal illness and plant disease. Yet the good my forefathers wrought is abiding, and if the Field is destroyed by housing estates, the soil they left will yield good gardens. There are many more 'comfortable words' than those Shakespeare used in fiction to rouse the passions of a city mob. In the quiet places it is possible to hope that any bit of good will live on.